STONE FOX BRIDE

# STONE ♥ FOX
## BRIDE

LOVE, LUST, AND WEDDING PLANNING
FOR THE WILD AT HEART

## Molly Rosen Guy

SPIEGEL & GRAU   NEW YORK

Published in the United States by Spiegel & Grau,
an imprint of Random House, a division of
Penguin Random House LLC, New York.

Spiegel & Grau and Design is a registered trademark of
Penguin Random House LLC.

Library of Congress Cataloging-in-Publication Data
Names: Guy, Molly, author.
Title: Stone fox bride : love, lust, and wedding
planning for the wild at heart / Molly Guy.
Description: First edition. | New York :
Spiegel & Grau, [2017] | Includes index.
Identifiers: LCCN 2016051557 | ISBN 9780812998092 |
ISBN 9780812998108 (ebook)
Subjects: LCSH: Weddings—Planning.
Classification: LCC HQ745 .G89 2017 |
DDC 392.5—dc23 LC record available at
https://lccn.loc.gov/2016051557

Printed in China on acid-free paper

randomhousebooks.com
spiegelandgrau.com

2 4 6 8 9 7 5 3 1

First Edition

For my parents,
the original Stone Fox Bride and Groom,
Ellen + Robert Rosen

# CONTENTS

STONE FOX BRIDE CLIENT
JESSICA THOMPSON
LOUNGING IN OUR GLENDA
DRESS AFTER SHE SAID, "I DO."

# WHAT THE FOX IS THE SFB BOOK?

WHEN I WAS PLANNING MY wedding, I couldn't find a single book that spoke to the amount of angst the whole process was giving me. They all used words like "playful updo" and were super chipper and prescriptive. Like: make the flowers look this way, plate the chicken that way, everything in this peppy, creepy tone that was kind of terrifying. Not my style—at all. In fact, the word "advice" sends a cold chill down my spine; it reminds me of my big sister yelling at me in middle school. I'm a sensitive, porous Pisces. If anyone ever tries to tell me what to do, I want to crawl under a rock. It's like: chill the eff out, stop shaking your finger in my face, and let's just sit down in a quiet café for coffee and a mellow convo. Maybe we'll get somewhere.

Interesting, honest, and generous women with great taste are my jam. In fact, they were the inspiration for the Stone Fox Bride brand from the start. My original goal was to create a retail space for creative gals to navigate the wedding industry from a place of authenticity. To find their dream dress in a mellow haven that basically felt like a living room. Then it became a collection of gowns. And then a blog. Then I was like: *Well, I might as well translate the whole thing into a book, so any bride out there can hop aboard the Fox Train and settle in for the ride.*

So if you're a bride-to-be, hopefully you'll find it helpful. Pick it up while you're peeing, skim it on the subway, blot your lipstick on its pages, then set it on fire while dancing in a satanic circle screaming "Destroy the Patriarchy" at the top of your lungs. You can also just close the whole thing now and read *Us Weekly* magazine. Whatever the fox you want.

—MOLLY ROSEN GUY

P.S.: Feel free to disregard my choice of (hopelessly heteronormative) pronouns throughout the text and substitute whatever words apply to your experience. Just 'cuz I appreciate a good penis, doesn't mean you have to.

# INTRODUCTION

A FOX TALE: HOW I FELL IN LOVE,
GOT MY LIFE (KIND OF) TOGETHER,
AND STARTED STONE FOX BRIDE

BEFORE I MET M, I was in single lady hell. I spent Valentine's Day at the local bookstore reading magazines. On my birthday I attended a media conference for Jewish people in Texas. I was on tons of Prozac, my best friends were my cats, and I had such bad sciatica that I sometimes walked with a cane. Evening activities included meditating, crying, and listening to "Landslide" on repeat. I remember looking at my BlackBerry one night before bed. It read "battery drained," which perfectly described my state of mind.

My dating life had been one disaster after another. If you took a look at my roster of boyfriends over the years, you would think I grew up in a highly dysfunctional broken home with cold, rude parents who never taught me a thing about love. Not so much. If my childhood was a movie montage, it would be a blurry haze of bushy hair and bellbottoms (Mom), big beard and Birkenstocks (Dad), and lots of Shabbat candles and cats and dogs and birthday parties and earnest talks post–Sunday stew about the importance of growing into a responsible Jewish woman of dignity and grace. Unfortunately, not much of it stuck.

Let's just say, the men I gravitated toward were not, as my mom would have liked, NJDs (nice Jewish doctors). They were often quite brutish, with criminal pasts and brown teeth. If one happened to use a condom or buy me a burrito I would sigh, "What a gentleman." Every now and then, a more socially acceptable suitor appeared, but for the most part, the cast of characters had many of the same traits as barn animals.

I had been through lots of breakups and boyfriends and felt super cynical about it all. There had been the hot-tempered TV actor with dyslexia and a '69 Dodge Dart. The tattooed fashion photographer who dangled my cat out the window. The other fashion photographer who called me "really fucking crazy"

PROUDLY SHOWING OFF MY CALIFORNIA TATTOO (WHICH HAS SINCE BEEN LASERED) IN THE EAST VILLAGE, 2003. RIGHT AFTER THIS PIC WAS SNAPPED, DAVID SPADE WALKED BY AND ASKED FOR MY NUMBER.

and threw fried calamari at my head. The comedian who cried during a BJ. The list goes on.

It took me a long time to get the memo that having crazy-electric chemistry with someone does NOT mean that person is your soulmate. Definitely take advantage of the feeling for a few weeks: have crazy sex while sobbing, tell him everything about your past, demand that he nurture your every tender emotional wound, then scream "Fuck you" wildly when he doesn't. But afterward, run away as fast as you can. You want to smear hot oil all over this man's penis in a dim-lit hotel room while laughing maniacally and blasting Kurt Cobain's version of "Where Did You Sleep Last Night"—not, for the love of Goddess, walk down the aisle on his arm.

My life since college had been a bummer. I moved to New York in my early twenties, convinced I was on my way to becoming the next It-Girl love child hybrid of Nancy Spungen and Carolyn Bessette-Kennedy. With a little Anaïs Nin, Holly Golightly, and Kim Basinger in 9½ Weeks mixed in, too. I'd live on pink cigs, red wine, and rare steak. I would wear ratty ball gowns, blue eyeliner, and big sunglasses. I would be on the cover of every magazine and Gwyneth Paltrow would be my best friend.

Unfortunately, this is NOT how it all went down. Every now and then I went through what seemed like a cool phase, but it never lasted, and for some reason I always ended up back on my couch watching *The Bachelor* and googling my name. Your twenties suck no matter where you live. But if you're crazy enough to move to Manhattan instead of doing Peace Corps or getting a normal job in a normal city, you have to have a certain amount of stupidity to survive.

Fast-forward to thirty-two years old. I was tired, depressed, and—quite literally—thought my life was over. On a yoga retreat a few months before I bonded with a blond actress who claimed she knew the secret to true love. Late at night, while our blissed-out fellow yoginis lay in *savasana* wearing linty leggings with vagina sweat circles, the actress lectured me sternly from the dining hall wearing a string bikini and Uggs. "Write down what you are looking for in a soulmate on a piece of paper," she instructed, dumping a small baggie of black herbs into a cup of cold tea. She said, "Goddess will be good to you, if you tell her what you want." But I didn't know what I wanted. I stared at that scrap of paper all night, was finally like, *Fuck this shit,* and went to bed. (Fine, the actress was Heather Graham, if you really want to know.)

Around that time, I got a message on Facebook: *Hey, I met you on the street with my friend Steve. –M.* I had no idea who this guy was or what he was talking about. Then I clicked on his photos. In every picture he was either racing a car or carving a turkey. There were lots of hunting rifles and helicopters. It looked like he wore hair gel. I was used to getting randomly asked out by creeps on Facebook—and was so over it all—that, in a moment of disgust and indignation, I deactivated my account then and there. The next day I told my friend Lisa about it on the subway: "This huge dork named M Facebooked me. Do you know him?" She was like, "Nope."

Six months later, Lisa told me that her friend had had lunch with M. "She said he was nice and cute," she reported back, which made my ears perk up. At that point, my prospects were so slim that "nice and cute" was the equivalent of saying: "Brad Pitt." Plus, the last date I had gone on had taken a terrible turn: after wining and dining me at a chic bistro in Chelsea, the Patrick Bateman–esque suitor brought me back to his apartment, ripped off my shirt, backed me up against the wall, and started spitting on my nipples. So I reactivated my Facebook account and sent M a message asking if he wanted to grab coffee. Literally

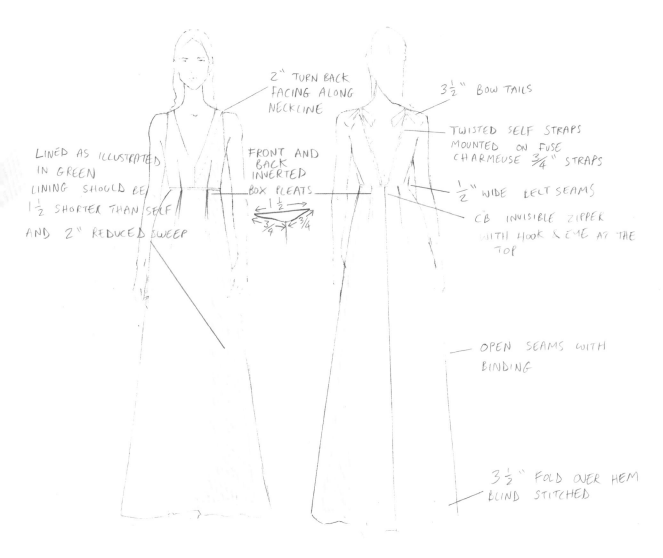

AN EARLY SKETCH OF OUR FARRAH GOWN

four seconds later the computer pinged: *Sure, when?* Accustomed to cruising rude scenesters who barely knew my name, I was both disgusted and intrigued by M's eager beaverness.

A few days later, we met at Mud café on Ninth Street. I had just come from babysitting and I was wearing draggy jeans, sneakers, and a pink T-shirt. I took a seat in the back, and a few secs later, in walked M. Nice, cute, short, fine. He was wearing a fleece and backpack on both shoulders. "I'm M," he announced and rubbed his chest. I was into his thick hair and grounded vibe but other than that was like, *whatever*. He told me he was a journalist, then launched into a hideously name-droppy series of celebrity stories that featured sexual intercourse with a Spice Girl, a rollerskating booze bender with Val Kilmer, how he used to clean Hunter S. Thompson's peacock cages in Colorado, and then that time Kurt Vonnegut, dripping in rain, mysteriously appeared at his desk and dropped a prose poem about jazz in his lap. Often the stories were punctuated with the phrase: "when I was an editor at *Rolling Stone*." He said that his penis was small and that he was poor and a hypochondriac, that he refused to touch doorknobs with his bare hands. At one point he stood up and said, "I have to whiz." We did bond over a shared love of Judy Blume and the fact that we didn't understand the Internet generation. Of all the people I know, I always thought I had the worst boundaries, but M's boundaries were so bad that he made me look like a repressed WASP. He gave me a piece of Trident on the walk home, and as we hugged outside my building, I said, "Thanks for the gum." When Lisa called later to ask how it had gone, I said, "He's fine, just a nice, short man." Then he called on the other line and asked if I wanted to see a movie on Saturday. I clicked back to Lisa and said, "He wants to see a movie, what should I say?" She said, "Do you have anything better to do?" I clicked back to M and said, "Sure, I guess."

We met outside the Sunshine Cinema on Houston Street two days later. M asked what I had been up to and I told him I had gone to an art opening earlier in the day. He said: "You do a lot of stuff, don't you?" And I said, "Yeah." And he asked, "Are you avoiding your life?" Suddenly, the light hit his eyes and I thought, *Whoa, he's deep and hot.* As we were walking into the theater, I noted that he was at least an inch taller than me. Before the movie he whispered if my parents were still married. I said yes, and that my grandparents were, too. M raised his eyebrows. I made a mental note: *Seems into marriage.* The lights dimmed and the movie started—in the first scenes Mexican gangsters climb aboard a train illegally to smuggle their way into the U.S. "When I was an editor at *Rolling Stone* I did that," M announced in a loud whisper, crunching on popcorn.

Afterward, we went to a restaurant on the Lower East Side, The Pink Pony, and sat at the bar. We started talking about books, one of my favorite subjects. I was in the middle of reading the Chris Farley book, and he'd just reread a biography of John Belushi. Turns out he was a pop culture and history nut and knew everything about everything. Major turn-on. Plus, I found myself staring intently at his wrists to ascertain what size his penis was. All of a sudden, the short dork had morphed into Paul Newman. Most guys I'd dated were tormented and creative and mean, but M was the first guy I'd met who was tormented and creative and nice—I was into it.

It was about ten at night and Ludlow Street with filling up with sexy twenty-somethings en route to the latest hip hot spot, and there we were, two sad sacks on a second date, sharing cake at the bar. At one point I remember saying, "I'm unhappy," and M said, "Me too." We both admitted that we felt uncool, past our primes. But none of it mattered because it seemed like we were in the middle of a conversation that we'd started years before. We kissed good night in the car ride home and I literally saw the words "my last first kiss" parade through my brain on a float. I ran inside my apartment, called Lisa and screamed, "He's the one." The next morning when I woke up, the world was a kind place.

That summer, M blew my mind. He took me to meet his parents in Maine and cooked me lobster over an open fire. We spent Saturday nights in bed watching old episodes of *M*A*S*H* with bowls of blueberries on our bellies. We camped

OUTTAKE FROM OUR FIRST LOOK BOOK, FALL 2012.

Upstate, rode horses in Oregon, went to a sweat lodge in Mexico, and climbed Machu Picchu. Once when I woke up in his Greenpoint apartment at four a.m. with a headache, he walked to the bodega in boxers to buy me aspirin. He always held my hand. No matter what dark piece of my past I threw at him, he was like, "Been there." Plus, his penchant for hyberbole kept me on my toes. Let's just say, the penis was far from small.

 I fell in love hard. It was deep and pure and perfect.

Eight months later, M asked me to marry him. It was midnight in February. We were having sex on the floor. There was no ring. That is the story.

BUT THEN what? All of a sudden I had a wedding to plan. And I had no idea where to start. Budget, flowers, food, dress . . . never once had I been that girl obsessed with Barbies and princesses and puffy pink things. When I was a kid, I spent my free time writing fan letters to V. C. Andrews and fantasizing about meeting Axl Rose in person. I had no idea where to start planning, and once I did, the pickings were slim. Eventually I patched together a beautiful wedding, but there was a bunch of stuff about the experience that I wasn't thrilled about. My dress was fine. The flowers . . . eh. Food: awesome; guests: amazing; and the ceremony was killer. It all came together in the end, but the process of creating it was frustrating and lonely.

Remember, this was 2009, the pre-Pinterest era. No one was talking about alternatives to the preppy white wedding. When I typed "bohemian bride" into Google, only a few blurry pics from the sixties popped up. On top of all this, I was working a corporate job at a cosmetics company—nothing like the cool career I'd always envisioned. Three weeks after I got married, I was eating dinner in Greenpoint with my friend Bronagh, and I said, "I have an idea for an alternative wedding dress shop." That conversation was the seed from which Stone Fox Bride grew.

My vision was simple: a sunny space full of faded rugs, plants, and, most important, a stylish selection of gowns, crowns, rings, and veils. The trouble was, every job I'd had up until that point had involved writing or editing—I had no background in fashion or business. I didn't know anything about . . . well, anything really. So I spent a few months reading books like *How to Start a Business* and *Retail for Dummies* and pretending to make a business plan. M still talks about the dreaded winter when I was dreaming up SFB, how I would lay on the couch crying and overwhelmed, watching *The Sopranos,* unopened books by billionaire entrepreneurs on the floor.

Eventually, I pitched the idea to my brother-in-law Peter, an entrepreneur who'd been in the music business for years. He became my partner and helped me raise money and guided me through mountains of paperwork. I found an office space on Craigslist and hired Bronagh's husband to transform it into a groovy oasis. Our desk was a huge wooden table sprouting cacti from the cracks.

Next came the actual dresses. I approached some local designers to see if they wanted to work with us. "What's the wedding dress you'd design for your best friend?" I'd ask. The results were wild—tie-dyed caftans with buttons down the back; knee-length shifts in purple silk satin tied with fat rope belts; a pink ombré halter gown with a crocheted smock top. I opened the showroom in February when I was six months pregnant. The first customer who walked in was named Jennifer Tee, a beautiful Amsterdam artist who ended up getting married in our Nomia brace dress.

But after that, no one bought anything! Brides would come in and they all loved the space and the concept, but not the dresses. They'd try them on, twirl around, and then ask if they could be made . . . in white! And with lace! Even the most punk chicks with floppy platinum bangs and tongue rings were requesting white dresses with lace overlays, and I didn't have anything for them. Months went by, and nothing was selling. So I decided to design a dress based on what our customers were always asking for: something simple, white, classic, and lacy. I found a patternmaker, sourced some fabric and brought it to a seamstress. I called it "the Molly" (it has since been renamed "the Polly"). It got swooped up the first day I hung it on the rack. So I designed a few more dresses—the Luisa (an all-lace knee-length shift), the Vivienne (a scoop neck champagne gown), the Lola (an open-back embroidered smock dress with pearl buttons). They started flying out of the store. Then we arranged to photograph the collection. Cass Bird shot it and Pam Love and Jemima Kirke modeled. It was a real *holy shit someone pinch me* experience. Jemima just had her second baby a month earlier and was standing in her undies and nursing bra in the middle of hair-and-makeup talking about breastfeeding, and Cass pulled in her assistant and our sales manager to model and they stripped down to their skivvies and stepped into our Chantilly

OUR FIRST CLIENT, ARTIST JENNIFER TEE, GOT MARRIED IN AMSTERDAM WITH SILK FLOWERS IN HER HAIR.

shift dresses, all the while Beyoncé blared and our florist-seamstress Rawan sat cross-legged on the floor hand-beading our cold-shoulder Cate gown.

I was happy that I'd been able to create the kind of gorgeous dresses I wished existed when I got married. But my clients had so many other questions that went beyond the gowns. The angst exceeded the wedding; it bled into all the compli-cated, emotionally intense situations that accompany love and marriage. They wanted to know if they had to change their names or whether to include their sisters-in-law in the planning process, and were they doomed if they didn't have sex on their wedding night. I talked to women who were freaked out about merg-ing finances with a partner saddled with massive amounts of credit card debt. Or brides who were dealing with mothers-in-law with mental illness. Sometimes it was smaller stuff, like the thought of a lifetime of dirty laundry on the floor of the shared bathroom. They would say: "This whole thing is a mindfuck, Molly—sometimes I miss being single!" I was a few years into my own marriage then, and could relate. My life with M resembled something in between *Happily Ever After* and *Reality Bites*.

During this time, we got a scary phone call from my in-laws. My father-in-law's routine checkup showed that he needed to have emergency bypass surgery STAT. In Boston. This all happened during one of the coldest winters in New York history. And, to be honest, driving to Boston from New York for the weekend was the last thing I felt like doing. Then I remembered the vows I'd written, and the line that said: "I will treat your family like my family." I'd said it in front of two hundred people. Whoops! Too late to take it back.

So I went. Nine hours there in a blizzard, eight hours back. Terrible traffic, terrible snowstorm.

Then the following weekend M wanted us to drive back to Boston. I wanted none of it. The thought of another seventeen hours in the car . . . I called a few girlfriends for their opinions, hoping someone would say: "Absolutely not! Take care of your own needs, obviously!" But no one did. Instead, they were like: "This is the deal. This is what you signed up for. You have to go." And they were right, although I wasn't happy about it. Not being able to do what I wanted to do, when I wanted to do it? There's a first time for everything, but let's just say—I was not a fan.

It turned out though that we really needed to be there. It was a scary weekend. The hospital unit where M's dad was recovering was a pretty rough place, and having both me and M in town to advocate on his behalf and support my mother-in-law was crucial. Let me emphasize the *both of us* part. In order for M to be able to fully support both his parents, I needed to be able to support *him*. That's a lot of what marriage is about, really. Showing up, shutting up, and giving unconditional love—even when you don't want to.

At the end of the day, the details of the wedding aren't even that significant. I still remember lots of them, of course: our tiered white cake layered with fresh cream, my nieces dancing around in dusty streams of sun during the reception, all my best friends in one room; my mom beaming down the aisle with a bow in her hair, and when my dad teared up on my arm before the ceremony started. But what stays most is the feeling I had driving away with M. Over the Pulaski Bridge and into the car wash on Manhattan Avenue. Just the two of us together, Bob Dylan on the radio, the smoky skyline of industrial Brooklyn against the October sky. My bare feet on the dash. How warm it was in the car.

# CHAPTER 1

# BLING IT ON

## THE LOWDOWN ON LOW-KEY PROPOSALS + RINGS

THE DAY AFTER M ASKED ME to marry him, I went to work at my fancy cosmetics job, where I was a copywriter. I remember it was a Friday, which meant that we were allowed to wear jeans! Yay! Huge deal. The office environment was super corporate and buttoned-up—we were definitely *not* encouraged to talk about the details of our personal lives.

Still, I couldn't resist sharing the news with my coworker.

"Guess what?" I whispered over the partition between our cubicles.

"What?"

"I'm engaged! We're getting married."

"Shut. Up."

She stood up fast, eyes wide, and grabbed my hand. Only there was nothing to see! My finger was totally naked.

"M didn't propose with a ring."

"What?"

"He just asked. There was no ring."

She sat back down, eyes on her computer screen.

"Mmm. Congrats."

And that was that.

Her reaction wasn't anomalous. The rest of the day, whenever I told someone the news, the first thing they'd do was grab my hand excitedly. But once they realized it lacked any bling, the conversation ended. It was almost like the proposal wasn't important. Shit, who cared about everlasting love if there was nothing sparkly to corroborate its existence!

I think M got the memo, because one week later, he got me a ring. From a pawn shop in Daytona, Florida . . . but a ring, nonetheless. He was with NASCAR driver Carl Edwards, shadowing him for a story. M is a car journalist and editor, which means that he's always traveling the world to report on races and drivers. He surprised me with the ring while I was getting a pedicure, got down on one knee, popped the question officially, and then we kissed. "You were shaking so much," he told me later. "So overcome with emotion." I didn't have the heart to tell him it was the spa massage chair set to HIGH!

The ring itself was not amazing. It was darling and sweet because M (and Carl) had picked it out, but the actual diamond—let's just say it was a teeny-tiny chip set in a super high prong and totally *not* my style. So a few weeks later, I asked M if he'd mind if I designed my own and he was fine with it. To be honest, I think what he said was "Sure, babe" with his eyes glued to a YouTube tutorial called "How to Smoke Meat."

So I set off for the diamond district to see what was available in my budget. My funds were limited. However, good Jewish girl that I am, I wanted a huge diamond. What to do? Thank God for raw grey diamonds, which are diamonds in their natural state. Uncut, un-polished, heavily imperfect, and much less expensive than their clear, polished counterpart. But still gorgeous. Once I discovered them, I was hooked! I found a loose diamond dealer who had a stash, then chose a five-carat one to set in rose gold pavé. When the ring finally materialized weeks later, it was stunning. And huge. And it didn't break the bank. Years later, I sold it to a Stone Fox Bride client. Now it's our signature piece. We remake it all the time and have sold dozens to Stone Fox grooms everywhere.

AFTER MY nana died, a beautiful, dusty emerald was among the jewelry dispersed among her eleven grandchildren. It sat in my jewelry box for several years, until I reset it in a vintage yellow gold setting—and used two diamond

RINGS BY MOCIUN

MY NANA AND GRANDPA, CAROLINE AND SOL ROSEN, AT THEIR CHICAGO WEDDING IN 1941. THEY WERE MARRIED FOR SIXTY-NINE YEARS AND DIED WITHIN SIX WEEKS OF EACH OTHER RIGHT BEFORE MY WEDDING.

earring studs as the side stones. I wore it for a year before I tucked it away and wore a vintage gypsy band for a while. After that I wore a Brazilian emerald ring that my friend Scosha designed for me, inlaid with my children's birthstones. Then I went back to Nana's emerald set with the two side stones and turned it into a solitaire with pavé and made the stones into two separate rings for my kids. I know I sound like a nut; I guess that the combination of not being a particularly sentimental person AND working in the wedding ring industry has made me pretty unattached when it comes to gems. I know this is unusual. I'm not saying that you, too, should adopt my *what-me-care* attitude when it comes to expensive heirloom pieces. But I do want you to keep in mind that it's just a ring! Just because he proposed with it, doesn't mean it's attached to your finger for the rest of your life.

# HIDDEN GEMS

### Jewelry Designer Anna Sheffield on Rose Gold, Coco Chanel, and Concentric Circles

**On the Coolest Ring She Ever Designed:** "I had a client who emailed me from Hong Kong requesting a custom engagement ring. He discovered me online and said that my 'classic with a twist' aesthetic seemed perfect for his girlfriend. I ended up creating an incredible five-carat emerald-cut diamond ring with beautiful trapezoid trillions on either side. It was deco-inspired and platinum and pavé all over. So pretty. We never even met in person."

**On the Second Coolest Ring She Ever Designed:** "I once made an engagement ring based on a painting someone had made—an abstract circle inside another circle. When she came for our appointment she brought the painting, and explained that it had been a gift to her girlfriend, that she had painted it to represent their love. I re-created the image in a concentric circle of tiny black and white diamonds with one slightly larger diamond accent in gold. I think the most beautiful thing about all engagement and ceremonial rings is what they end up meaning to the people who give them to each other. In this case, the couple knew so well what that symbol was for them—and it was a joy to take this kind of approach in the way I design."

**On Stones + Metals:** "I love working with rose and yellow gold. Gold is incredibly reflective—ancient Mayan mirrors were actually made out of gold. It's such a beautiful material and it's wonderful to solder and form."

**On Designing a Ring for Her Fantasy Bride:** "I would love to make Coco Chanel's wedding ring. She was such a beast—she came from nothing and she worked so hard to change people's ideas of what women were allowed to do. The center stone would definitely be a black pearl."

## ON BENDED KNEE? NO NEED.

We've all heard the cupcakes-and-champagne proposal stories, but let's take some pressure off ourselves here—fireworks and flash bombs be damned! The assumption seems to be that the more thought and preparation that goes into the proposal, the more he adores you. That's just not true. Plenty of amazing couples get engaged very quietly. To be honest, I kind of prefer it that way. My dad and mom got engaged over a breakfast of bacon and eggs at a diner. I think the conversation went something along the lines of my dad saying, "We should probably think about getting married," and my mom replying, "Yeah, we probably should." They've been together for forty-five years.

MY CUTE HIPPIE PARENTS AT THEIR TEENY 1971 WEDDING. "ON THE WAY TO THE CEREMONY," SAYS MY MOM, "WE GOT STONED."

LIFE IS A PARTY

DRESS LIKE IT

WHY NOT NOW?

STONE FOX
BRIDE

Just because your wedding is like, right around the corner, doesn't mean you can:

* Call your mother-in-law a cunt to your fiance's face
* Take more than one Klonopin to sleep because "you have NO idea, the stress"
* Max out your credit card at Isabel Marant
* Not be an amazing friend to all your amazing friends who suffered through your obsessive texts and phone calls and freak-outs during the falling-in-love process, when you were convinced the man you are about to marry was going to lose interest and/or your number
* Drop more than five pounds, do colonics, binge
green juice

## Fine Jeweler Soraya Silchenstedt on Pink Diamonds, Platinum, and Marilyn Monroe

**On the Coolest Ring She Ever Designed:** "One of my closest friends went through a bad breakup and she asked me to design a ring for her. She was having a really hard time so I wanted to make something that was protective and empowering and that would bring her good fortune. I came up with a moonstone and diamond cabochon ring. Moonstone is a luminous gem that attracts peaceful energy and brings balance."

**On Her Favorite Couple:** "I designed a ring for my friend's girlfriend who is a singer. He sent me a link to her music and we spent six months talking on the phone about all the things he loved about her, trips they had taken to the Caribbean, and their meditation practice. We ended up making a pear-shaped diamond in a platinum setting. We wanted it to feel strong and delicate—like diamond strings on a harp."

**On Stones + Metals:** "I love working with platinum. I love the color—it's not too bright and it's not too dull. Also, it's soft and malleable so you can set softer stones in it, like emeralds. It has more flexibility than rose or white gold. I'm also in love with natural pink diamonds. I don't like synthetic stones . . . I would rather use a slightly flawed stone than a treated one."

**On Designing a Ring for Her Fantasy Bride:** "I wish I could have made a ring for Marilyn Monroe—something beautiful and simple that would have made her feel understood—something to give her a glimmer of hope. Maybe a thin pink diamond band. She wore a lot of big jewelry in her films—but once you stripped everything away she was very delicate and understated."

# Jewelry Designer Kathryn Bentley on Luminescence, Masculinity, and Matching Bands

**On the Coolest Ring She Ever Designed:** "The first engagement ring I made was inspired by a Georgian man's ring that belonged to my tattoo artist friend. It was super masculine, yet it was beautiful and antique. My design was a luminescent octagon ring made with a rose-cut diamond, mounted as a solitaire, with a triangle of blue opal and pavé diamonds on each side, acting as the stone's eyes."

**On Her Dream Ring:** "If I were to get married I would wear a classic gold wedding band and I would want it to match my partner's. Understated, durable, timeless—a perfect representation. There is truly nothing as chic as a European couple in matching thin bands."

**On Stones + Metals:** "I generally look at different movements in art and jewelry and textiles and then hone in on it and reinterpret it with my own hand. I'm not a girly girl—I don't give a rat's ass about anything sparkly or blingy. I love beautiful, artistic creations that look like they were sculpted with integrity."

**On Designing a Ring for Her Fantasy Bride:** "I'd love to create matching bands for Susan Sontag and Annie Leibovitz. I'd hand-carve simple gold bands and line the interior with tiny diamonds."

## BLOOD FROM A STONE

Is that weird movie starring Leonardo DiCaprio the extent of your knowledge about blood diamonds? Read on for tips on how to ensure that the gem on your finger was sourced with integrity.

*An ethical stone is one that:*

• Has not financed a civil war. (Historically, blood diamonds or conflict diamonds are stones mined in war zones and sold to finance war efforts. Diamonds mined during civil wars in Sierra Leone, Liberia, and the Republic of Congo have been given the label.)

• Did not, in the process of mining, disrupt the environment, use child labor, or compromise the safety of workers.

• Went through the Kimberley Process (named after a city in South Africa) and is certified "conflict-free."

Word to the wise: If the person who sold you your stone is not able to provide information and paperwork about the stone's origins, then chances are it was not sourced ethically.

## TWINKLE TWINKLE

Gemologist Olivia Landau recommends having your ring cleaned by a professional jeweler at least once a year. "If you have micro-pavé all around the diamond," she says, "get it checked every six months to make sure everything is tight and secure. In addition to getting it professionally cleaned once or twice a year, clean your ring at home with a toothbrush and mild soap. I would also advise against excessive use of hand lotion because you can end up with gross buildup in the crevices."

# ROLLING STONES: A CAUTIONARY TALE

You know that idyllic image we all conjure up of the shiny satin pillow topped with two bands, tenderly carried down the aisle by an adorable kid? Isn't that the first thing that comes to mind when you hear the words "ring bearer"? Stone Fox Bride Julie Schumacher Grubbs's mom thought the same thing. Her tiny vintage diamond pavé band was tied to a hand-sewn ring pillow with white embroidery and satin ribbons. But three minutes before the ceremony the ring slipped off and was nowhere to be found. "It was surreal," says Julie. "It happened really fast." After multiple flashlight searches, the band never turned up. "The experience sucked," she says, "but it happened for a reason. It helped my husband and me figure out how we react in a crisis. In the end we just accepted it and didn't freak out."

JULIE AND HER HUSBAND, MIKE, AT THEIR NEW ORLEANS WEDDING

# IT'S A HARD ROCK LIFE

*These Three Diamonds Had a Rough Start.*

### IT WAS A BUTTON ON A TUXEDO

"My husband Ben's great-grandfather worked for a bank and was a state senator in Pennsylvania. He also owned a white tie tuxedo that had five-carat diamonds for each of the buttons. When the Depression hit, he lost everything and had the diamonds made into rings." —JENNY SEDLIS

### SLIPPED INTO THE SEINE

"Chris proposed to me in the grass under the Eiffel Tower. The next afternoon as we were having drinks, the ring slipped off my finger into the Seine. He dove into the thirty-eight-degree water but couldn't find it! Eventually the fire department showed up. Fifteen French firemen and two scuba divers searched all night long until they found it."
—KRISTEN HYERS

### THE STONE SURVIVED NAZI GERMANY; HIS FAMILY DIDN'T

"The diamond belonged to my grandfather who lived in a Polish shtetl with his wife and two daughters. When the Nazis came into power, he was hidden by a poor pastor. Eventually he fled, leaving behind the ring, but returned after the war and discovered the pastor still had it in his possessions. My grandfather was the only one of his immediate family to survive Auschwitz. He moved to America, remarried, and had children. One of them was my mother, who wore it as a necklace for forty years. —ALEX WOOLFSON

# WILL YOU MARRY ME?

A FEW MONTHS AFTER SFB OPENED I STARTED TAKING PICTURES OF MY CLIENTS' RINGS AND ASKING THEM THE DETAILS BEHIND THEIR PROPOSALS. SOON WOMEN FROM ALL OVER THE WORLD STARTED SUBMITTING THE STORIES THROUGH EMAIL AND INSTAGRAM. FIVE YEARS LATER, WE'VE AMASSED OVER FOUR THOUSAND ORIGINAL STORIES. CHECK 'EM OUT AT @STONEFOXBRIDE/#STONEFOXRINGS.

PROPOSED IN THE MIDDLE OF THE ICE SKATING RINK. #STONEFOXRINGS

AT THE METROPOLITAN MUSEUM OF ART. #STONEFOXRINGS

HE BEGGED. #STONEFOXRINGS

GOT DOWN ON ONE KNEE ON A TRAIN LEAVING BALTIMORE STATION. #STONEFOXRINGS

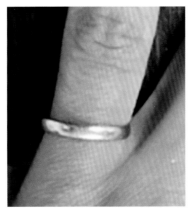

SHE WAS TWO MONTHS PREGNANT. HE INSCRIBED IT WITH "BTS": BEAT THE SYSTEM. #STONEFOXRINGS

AFTERWARD THEY JUMPED IN THE OCEAN. #STONEFOXRINGS

THEY WERE SAILING IN THE BAHAMAS, DRINKING BEER. #STONEFOXRINGS

THEY WERE ON A WALK WITH THEIR YOUNGEST CHILD. #STONEFOXRING

AT 11:11 HE SAID, "MAKE A WISH." #STONEFOXRINGS

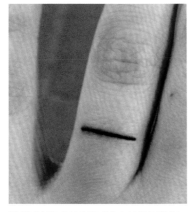

PROPOSED ON TOP OF A MOUNTAIN. #STONEFOXRINGS

DRINKING CHAMPAGNE ON THE BALCONY OF AN OLD MANSION. #STONEFOXRINGS

ON A YOGA SURF RETREAT IN COSTA RICA. #STONEFOXRINGS

# THE BEST BLING FOR YOUR BUDGET

## HOW TO CHOOSE A RING AT ANY PRICE POINT

Let's be honest: at the end of the day, budget is the factor that determines the ring that ends up on your finger. Some guys adhere to the weird dogma (which actually comes from a De Beers ad campaign) that says the ring must cost two months' salary, some propose with a family heirloom, some couples decide on a ring together, and some—as in my case—get engaged with no ring at all. My advice? Don't stress. Your engagement ring is just a piece of jewelry—not a reflection of class, status, or prestige. And it will be gorgeous, no matter how much you choose to spend.

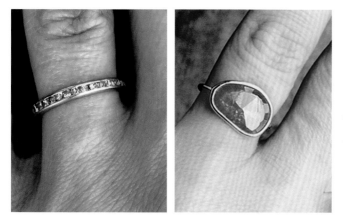

**If your budget is $1,500 or less:** Go with a thin band in rose, white, or yellow gold or platinum, and have it engraved. Slice rings are also gorgeous, and you can do a sapphire, ruby, or raw diamond. Never underestimate simplicity.

**If your budget is $2,500 or less:** Go with a beautiful diamond under .5 carats with accent stones. There are also semiprecious gemstones such as aquamarine, morganite, tourmaline, or white sapphire in this price range. Complement a smaller stone with milgrain on the band or a

unique asymmetrical setting. You can also get a simple pavé band in white diamonds, black diamonds, emeralds, rubies, or sapphires.

**If your budget is $5,000 or less:** I love a good raw grey diamond ring. Raw grey or brown diamonds come in a range of shades and can have cool inclusions that change the color and make the stone unique. Nothing beats a spectacular teardrop-faceted raw grey diamond in a prong or bezel setting.

**If your budget is $7,500:** There are some gorgeous rings available at this price point that have a cool old story and pack a serious punch. Think an art deco ring from the thirties with a .60-carat diamond center stone and sapphire accents. Alternately, consider adding a pavé halo to a raw grey diamond.

**If your budget is $10,000 or above:** One word: Victorian. A vintage Victorian pink gold ring with engraving on the band and an old English-cut one-carat center stone. Perfection.

**If your budget is $18,000 or above:** Go for a sensational oval-cut diamond, a marquise solitaire, a cool emerald with asymmetrical diamond baguettes, or the eternally classic clear one-carat white diamond solitaire in a prong setting with a thin gold or platinum band.

# ON THE BRIGHT SIDE

After my nana died, my aunt Joyce inherited her truly sick, truly massive, nearly flawless five-carat round cut diamond ring. Believe me, I was not happy about it, but hey—Joyce was her first and only daughter, so there was only so much of a JAP-py tantrum I could throw. In all seriousness, it was a stunning ring that Nana wore every day, and I was happy to know that it was still getting airtime out there in the universe . . . that is, until Joyce looked down at her hands one day, mid–washing dishes, and discovered that the prongs were holding, literally, nothing. Screams, tears, phone calls, retracing of steps ensued, but alas . . . the diamond never reappeared. I know it's a bleak story, but she made peace with it and so have I.

The truth is, once you put a precious gem on your finger and step out in the world, the whole thing is basically out of your hands (no pun). Still, that's never deterred most gals from being a sucker for some serious sparkle.

Just don't forget to insure that motherfucker.

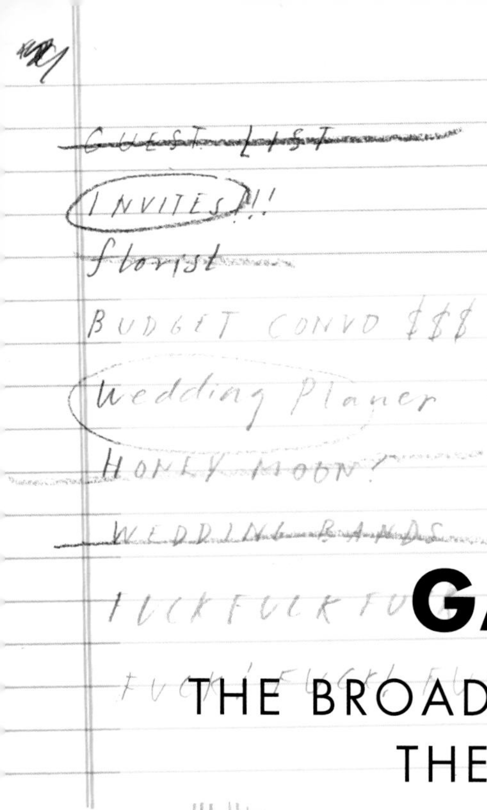

# CHAPTER 2

# GAME PLAN

## THE BROAD-STROKES BLUEPRINT FOR THE ANTI-BRIDEZILLA

INVITES!!

florist

BUDGET CONVO $$$

Wedding Planner

HONEY MOON?

NO MATTER
NEVER MIND
NO MIND
NEVER MATTER

EITHER WAY IT WORKS
35 90

with a [...]
that was
MORE then
LOVE.

dear Allen

LIFE IS A PARTY

DRESS LIKE IT

STONE FOX
BRIDE

Just because your wedding is like, right around the corner, doesn't mean you can:
* Call your mother-in-law a cunt to your fiance's face
* Take more than one Klonopin to sleep because "you have NO idea, the stress"
* Max out your credit card at Isabel Marant
* Not be an amazing friend to all your amazing friends who suffered through your obsessive texts and phone calls and freak-outs during the falling-in-love process, when you were convinced the man you are about to marry was going to lose interest and/or your number
* Drop more than five pounds, do colonics, binge and purge, or only drink green juice
* Lose sight of the time when you were single, struggling, and scared, and your dating life was a drama and a disaster, drunken dinners and miserable makeouts, and walks-of-shame home at dawn holding your underwear, and a cigarette, and a heaviness in your heart, convinced life would always be an endless lonely night spent in a studio apartment crowded with cats, tabloids and tears.
* Throw out the hot slut dress the tattooed photog tore off you when you cornered him after-hours in an alley with a head of ratted ringlets and a smeary smoky eye
* Press snooze more than once every morning
* Pray your maid-of-honor doesn't look prettier than you
* Google your ex while your husband-to-be is asleep
* Call in sick then spend the day in bed on FB
* Take an exercise class more than once a day that has the word "soul", "fly", or "core" in it
* Forget your good fortune, or the fact that, as a STONE FOX BRIDE, it is your duty to be kind, cool, and beautiful in all forms — and to honor the women before you who took this leap of faith, too — from your Nana, to your Mom, to Bianca Fucking Jagger — and to have Love, do Love and be Love — because that's really all there is.

In foxiness forever,

IF it DOSEN'T MATTER
[...] IT

# WEDDING PLANNING 101

WHEN IT COMES TO COORDINATING events, I'm pretty lazy, so I had to ask my wedding planner, Xochitl Gonzalez, creative director of a downtown NYC events company, AaB Creates, to basically write this section of the book. Check out her step-by-step guide below.

**1. Do nothing.** Just 'cuz the ring is on your finger doesn't mean that you have to start planning the wedding right away! Savor that freshly engaged feeling and try to ignore the expectations of family members and friends. "Enjoy the fact that you've decided to make this commitment without getting obsessed with the party," says Xochitl. "Just be engaged for at least two months."

**2. Decide on a date.** Six to twelve months is the ideal amount of time to plan a wedding. Choose a time of year that you love. If you're a winter person, do not have a summer wedding. If your younger brother is graduating from college in May, don't get married in May! Consider family milestones and important events in your friends' lives. "You want everyone you love to be there," says Xochitl.

**3. Identify family members who don't annoy the shit out of you.** It's important to delegate, but don't make everything a group decision. You should pick and choose when you want input from family or friends. Dress shopping can be a great way to bond with the women in your family. Choosing food can be fun for everyone—and a great time to involve Dad. "A sibling you are close to and who gets you can be a great person to bounce ideas off and confide in when things get tricky," says Xochitl. "But consider where they are in their life. If your sister has recently gone through a breakup or expressed some jealousy about your upcoming nuptials, she might not be the best wingwoman."

**4. Sort out budget expectations.** Have a candid (and likely uncomfortable) conversation with your fiancé about money. Keep the judgment out of it and stick to the numbers. Only involve your parents if they are helping you out financially. According to Xochitl, "If your parents are contributing, you need to establish what they expect in exchange. No one wants to say it out loud, but the person paying for the wedding is naturally going to have a lot of say in how the money gets spent. If you want to call all the shots, you should probably put up all the money. Get on the same page with your fiancé about what you both envision and figure out what you realistically can afford. If you want a big, lavish affair in a grand hotel, it may not be realistic to do it in an expensive city like LA, New York, or DC. If you want everyone you love to attend, you may have to choose a more accessible city. This is also the time to talk about a prenup. Basically if you're inheriting or have inherited family money or you have your own business, you should meet with a prenup lawyer to get something drafted. Broach the conversation by saying, 'Babe, I love you so much, and I will always love you, even if

things don't work out between us. No matter what happens, I never want to fight about money.' "

**5. The guest list.** Another long convo with your partner alert! Take a deep breath and start talking head count. If the venue has very limited space or you need to be selective for financial reasons, chances are Third Cousin Mo won't make the cut. It's okay to keep that shit lean—no need to invite the coworker from your first job who you used to smoke cigs with in the stairwell. Once you get clear on who's coming, kill two birds with one fox and send out your save-the-dates digitally, along with a request for the guests' home addresses.

**6. Wedding planner: yay or nay?** "If you want to feel like a guest at your own wedding and you want your friends and family to feel like guests at your wedding (instead of DIY helpers), you'll probably want to budget for a day-of/month-of wedding planner," says Xochitl. "This cost can range from anywhere between $750–$5,000, depending on the planner's experience and the level of service you'd like. A good question when first interviewing a potential planner is: 'What is the average budget you work with?' If you have room in your budget and you know you want more help, you might want to consider hiring a full-service planner. Think of the decision to hire a wedding planner the same way you think about deciding to dye your hair at home versus dying it at a salon—or the decision between decorating your own apartment versus hiring an interior designer."

**7. Mood that board.** Identify what kind of wedding you want to have: rustic barn, mellow beach, urban chic, you get the drift. Have no idea where to start? Think about what kinds of things, no matter how insignificant they seem, resonate with you. Before I planned my wedding I had no idea where to begin—only that I wanted my wedding to feel cozy and chic like Sunday brunches at Nana's house when I was a kid. That was my starting-off point, and my reference point for the menu, décor, and vibe. And don't forget to Pin. "The best way to figure out your style is to search all the categories of Pinterest for inspiration," says Xochitl. "Don't just look at other wedding boards. Look at album covers, look at artwork, look at restaurants, look at interior design mags. Pin a lot of not-wedding stuff on your board first that resonates with you. Then fill it in with wedding stuff you like—

THE MOOD BOARD ABOVE MY DESK

mainly flowers, chairs, locations, and dresses." And trust your intuition. You know more about what you want than you think you do.

**8. Book your professionals.** "Decide on the big-ticket stuff first," says Xochitl. "Book the venue. Then book the DJ or band. Next decide on a caterer, a cake, and any rentals. This stuff is expensive and you want to budget accordingly. Next book a photographer and/or videographer, and a florist. Save the smaller décor decisions for last. You want to have the bases covered before turning to the details. Make sure each vendor provides you with a contract that lays out the terms of what happens in case you need to cancel."

**9. The ceremony.** Start looking around for officiants who can deliver the kind of ceremony you want. This will require at least one conversation with your partner, preferably after a BJ, because at this point, aren't all these logistics kind of a drag? Shaman, rabbi, priest, yoga teacher . . . (see chapter 8). They book up quickly, and some of them require multiple meetings before agreeing to help you seal your deal. Of course, if you can't be bothered, pick a friend who has a charismatic personality and a penchant for public speaking, then have them get ordained on the Internet and call it a day.

**10. Invitations.** "If you love paper, by all means have someone design something awesome for you, and send it six to nine weeks in advance (twelve weeks if you didn't do a save-the-date)," says Xochitl. Obviously the farther in advance you send it, the higher your yield. So if you want to really not have a lot of your annoying extended family come, maybe you send it exactly six weeks before and

hope a lot of them are busy. "Digital, however, is awesome," she says. "It's easy for people to retrieve, enables you to collect RSVPs, and it's good for the environment."

**11. Plan the other parties.** "Don't bother having an engagement party if your wedding is less than nine months away," says Xochitl. "Put that money into your wedding. If you want your friends to throw you a bachelorette party, give them parameters. Like: 'I don't want to do Vegas.' Ideal timing for a bachelorette party is two to three months before the wedding, but make sure you spread out your bachelorette party from your shower, if you are having one. You don't want people to get resentful about having to shell out money for you every few months. The day-after wedding brunch is not really necessary, either. Save your money and do something for your guests the night before the wedding, such as a rehearsal dinner or welcome drinks."

**12. Honeymoon.** Decide where you want to go and how much you want to spend. Before settling on a destination for your getaway, discuss what you want out of your first trip as husband and wife. Ever consider that you two might have separate notions of what a relaxing vacay actually is? I, personally, am the type that likes to spend my time off on a beach with a bunch of books and a coconut with a straw sticking out. My husband, on the other hand, can't stand sitting for more than ten minutes. If funds are slim, don't underestimate the power of the Internet. You can crowdsource as part of your gift registry or cut costs by doing an apartment swap. Costa Rica, Paris, Laos, New Mexico . . . options start opening up when you think outside the fox. The whole be-a-tourist-in-your-own-city sounds a little cheesy, but staycations can actually be really fun. Why not hole up in a hotel room and still make it to work on Monday morning? Or just start saving. I know lots of couples that don't take their honeymoon until a year or two after the rings are on their fingers.

# FOUR WOMEN, FOUR WAYS OF PLANNING A WEDDING

TIME WAS NOT ALWAYS OF THE ESSENCE FOR THESE FOXY BRIDES.

### Bonnie McLean on Excel Spreadsheets, Sunny Weather, and "Sweet Caroline"

**On Planning:** "I never considered taking less than a year to do it—that just seemed like a given. Also, I live in California but the wedding was in Wisconsin, so it required a lot of traveling back and forth. A lot of Excel spreadsheets. It also helped that I worked with a wedding producer and florist who fully got my vision. I wanted a lot of mossy green colors and mason jars. I know that these days 'mason jar' is a bad word but in 2008 they were considered super cool and offbeat."

**On Her Fiancé's Involvement:** "He really cared about the music. He used to be a DJ and had strong feelings about what songs should and shouldn't be played. In fact, he gave the DJ a 'Do Not Play' List—'Sweet Caroline' was at the top of it. He thinks it's the most generic song. In the end, we actually paid the DJ extra to stay longer and the whole thing turned into a wild dance party. I hadn't exactly envisioned myself fist-pumping to 'Living on a Prayer' at my wedding, but what can you do."

**On Praying to the Weather Gods:** "I'm not by nature a stressed-out person, but worrying about the weather became a full-time job. I looked at the *Farmers' Almanac* constantly. I had my heart set on a beautiful outdoor wedding, but up until three days before it looked like heavy thunderstorms. Another girl I knew had an outdoor wedding in Wisconsin and there was literally a monsoon on her wedding day. She forgot to put the flooring down on the tent and all the guests were slipping and sliding around in the grass and covered in mud."

**On the Day Of:** "The weather was perfect—sunny and blissful. We were married in front of a lake and during the wedding herons flew overhead and then started skimming the water. We had a Jewish ceremony, and at one point the rabbi said, 'Look out at your friends and family and see the warmth of the community around you.' I did, and that just meant the world to me."

# Katerina Caliva on Shamans, Mariachis, and Mexico

**On Eloping:** "We decided to get married three days before leaving for a vacation to Mexico. Two of our close friends were coming with us and everything just seemed to fall into place. We didn't want to deal with planning a party and food, all that stuff gives me anxiety. I've never cared about getting married and I don't like being the center of attention."

**On What She Wore:** "I already had a vintage Mexican wedding dress in my closet and the day before we left, I bought a little pearl headpiece to wear with it."

**On the Celebration:** "My husband found a mariachi band through a local event planner. He also arranged a shaman to marry us in a ceremony that focused on wind, sea, earth, and sky. At the end, we threw flowers into the wind to signify being carried along together forever. Afterward we went back to our hotel and partied with our friends 'til five a.m."

**On the Aftermath:** "When we got home we wrote an email to everyone we knew telling them that we'd gotten married, attaching a photo from our ceremony. Some people expressed disappointment to have missed it, but since the whole thing was unplanned, they didn't feel deliberately excluded. We thought it was very democratic to tell them all at the same time."

## Shelly Lynch-Sparks on Pool Parties, Sunset Cocktails, and Planning a Wedding in Puerto Rico

**On Deciding to Go Destination:** "We got engaged right around the time that gay marriage was legalized in New York and we knew that with our budget of 60K, we'd only be able to throw a mediocre party in Manhattan. So we decided to go destination and plan a four-day party where we could feed our guests and get them drunk every single day. We had a soft spot for Puerto Rico because we got engaged there."

**On Managing Details from Far Away:** "There were so many things I didn't consider in advance, like where to get ice from and how to keep drinks cold. I booked our caterers by looking on wedding blogs. I dug around and found two people who got married on the same island before us, then I googled their vendors and called them up."

**On Getting the Guests There:** "There was a backlash once people heard they were going to have to travel. But then I designed and sent out a vintage letterpress postcard detailing all of the festivities—the rehearsal dinner, pool party, beach party, wedding, and sunset farewell cocktails. A lot of people who initially said they couldn't come changed their minds when they realized how fun it was going to be. We were very organized about everything. We didn't want anyone to be anywhere without a drink in their hand and plenty to eat at all times. We also hired a day-of planner, which made the day stress-free. We didn't have to lift a finger to do anything other than drink champagne."

## Chi Kim Planned Her Wedding in Three and a Half Weeks So That Her Terminally Ill Mother Could Be by Her Side

**On Wedding Planning:** "We were originally going to have a full year of planning, but after Jesse proposed, I found out that my mom's cancer had progressed. She only had a few more months to live. So we pulled everything together in about three and a half weeks. And it ended up being incredibly special and memorable. I had quit my job to take care of her, which actually gave me time to plan the wedding. If I'd been working full-time, it would have been impossible. My husband and I are very like-minded in our tastes and the direction that we wanted to go in, and since we didn't have time to labor over decisions, if something looked great, we just went with it. What holds our relationship together today is the partnership we formed when my mom was sick. It was the beginning of learning to build our own family and make decisions under pressure."

**On Designing a Dress Last Minute:** "I only had a month, so I worked with a patternmaker I knew through friends. Two nights before the wedding, I was in the depths of Brooklyn with the patternmaker, her dressmaker in her living room, making final adjustments. The next morning I realized there was a big crease in the front that had been pressed in. During the whole planning process I'd managed to keep my cool, but that was my, for lack of a better word, 'bridezilla' moment. I was near tears. I didn't know what to do, because I was hours away from getting married and there was this big crease. So my dear friend came to the rescue. He met me at the hair salon and ran to Bed Bath & Beyond during my appointment and purchased a hand steamer."

**On Laughter and Tears:** "Our ceremony was really emotional. Everyone was crying. We spoke about my mom. We spoke about mothers. I mean, you need to talk about it. For the reception, my mother and her sister had made these special Korean hors d'oeuvres with Korean hot sauce to dip them in. The staff at our venue was supposed to lay it all out. But they put the food out without the hot sauce, and my friends just went for it. All my friends were going up to my mom to tell her how delicious the hors d'oeuvres were, but all she could talk about was how no one was eating them with the hot sauce! I had to remind the crew to bring it out. One of my closest girlfriends that I've known since I was sixteen and I were cracking up about it. It was a relief to laugh after such an emotionally charged ceremony."

**On Serendipity:** "We were about to leave for our big dance party when one of our guests came running in to tell us that another wedding party was releasing paper lanterns into the sky just outside our event space. We released a lantern of our own and posed with the other newlyweds. It was one of those wonderful, spontaneous New York moments. From there we went to The Wooly in the Woolworth Building a few blocks north and danced the night away with our nearest and dearest. My mom had gone home to bed by then, but she had a ball, which was the happiest part of one of the happiest days of my life."

# STAND YOUR GROUND

I can think of no greater hell than trying to plan your wedding to please other people, at the expense of your own vision. You can never make everyone happy and you will make yourself miserable in the process. Maybe it sounds a bit strange to talk about your authentic self when it comes to your wedding; after all, what does authenticity have to do with choosing flowers and tablecloths and rental chairs? But here's the deal: Your wedding is all about you and your partner. It should be a day that's devoted to your love and commitment and the union you are creating. It's about celebrating the official start of your life together, with all of the people you love surrounding you and sending you good vibes. It's about creating an event that looks and feels as joyful as the love you feel in your heart.

There are probably a lot of people who care what your wedding looks like. Maybe your mother-in-law is a stern posh WASP who loves monogrammed china, while you're all about fish tacos and thrift store linens. Maybe your sister is a radical feminist who finds the idea of a bride wearing white to be a revolting heteronormative trope designed to turn modern women into meek virginal lambs while all you've ever wanted is to walk down the aisle in a creamy caftan. Maybe your best friend thinks that beach weddings are tacky, but ever since you were a wee fox you've wanted to exchange your vows in the sand. Whatever the disagreement, sometimes it's tempting to just avoid conflict. Believe me, I get it. I'm a people-pleasing second child and I would much rather shut the fuck up and go with the flow than deal with the discomfort of asserting myself and being all, "No, bitch. It's my way or the highway." But unless you're a billionaire heiress socialite who regularly has parties thrown in her honor, this is your one time to own it. Speak your truth and do you—no one else can.

# CHAPTER 3

# DON'T STRESS THE DRESS

## IT'S OKAY TO SAY NO WAY TO THE WHITE WEDDING GOWN

DRESSING UP GIVES ME ANXIETY. A lot of the decisions I've made in my life—from what restaurant to choose to what career to pursue—have been based on whether or not I can wear jeans. I can probably count on two hands the number of times I've gotten dressed up. There was my 1994 junior prom outfit: I went braless in a beige slip with cork platforms. My date and I partied afterward at a Chicago Marriott blasting "Sympathy for the Devil" 'til we got busted by hotel security. Then there was senior prom, when I skipped the footwear altogether and went barefoot in a ratty muumuu that showcased my hairy armpits. Prom started at seven and by eleven I was wandering, stoned with Sean Timbo, down Michigan Avenue. When I was a junior in college, I wore an old kimono with orthopedic shoes to an Oscar party high in the Hollywood Hills. At the time, I thought Matt Dillon was making eyes at me from across the room. But he probably just thought I was a mental patient on the run.

My wardrobe staples: a granddad cardigan tossed over a threadbare blouse. Tattered nightie beneath too-tight sweater. Secondhand psychedelic Indian sack with torn holey hems dragging down the subway stairs. Mostly I'm a jeans and tee girl. My mom and sister, for as long as I can remember, have pleaded with me to *please look chic*. Find clothes that fit. Buy a padded bra. Buy a bra, period.

A few weeks after M proposed, my mom flew in from Chicago to go dress shopping. That morning, I strapped on my Converse and rode the 6 train to a swanky uptown wedding showroom to meet her and my sister. Mom is a poetry-reading, chunky-necklace-wearing, dried-bean-hoarding, self-described cat whisperer. Shopping's not her thing, unless it's for Chinese herbs. But Becca—from the depths of her Intermix-obsessed, pink cashmere–clad heart—is obsessed with clothes. She'd made the appointment at the uptown place, where she'd bought her own wedding dress ten years before.

Within minutes, I found myself standing in my underwear in a tiny torture chamber of a dressing room reeking of talcum. When I described my vibe as "Manson family" to the woman helping me, she looked like she'd been shot. Then she disappeared into the back and returned with a tight lace column, very Miss America. I zipped it up, stepped out of the dressing room, and approached the wall of mirrors. As I prepared a monologue on how my identity felt subjugated by the dominant paradigm, Becca and Mom started nodding and clasping their hands.

"This is it!" They high-fived.

No, thank you.

I tried on four more dresses, all heinous straitjackets with ruffles, then we went out for chopped salads. Bec and Mom claimed that they loved every dress I'd tried on, which annoyed me to no end. I knew they were in a rush to get the whole thing over with so they could nap.

After lunch, we headed downtown to a different showroom that I'd chosen. Much more my speed. The dresses were flowy with not a cupcake skirt in sight. The second or third one I tried on was a diaphanous caftan with huge sleeves and beadwork. When I came out of the dressing room I found my mom lying supine on a chaise, phone to her ear, talking to my dad about their cat's homeopath while Bec hijacked my dressing room to try on a blue jumpsuit from the bridesmaid's rack. Mom hung up with Dad, gave me the once-over, grimaced, and said, "Reminds me of your prom dress."

I looked in the mirror. She was right. It looked like the muumuu from senior year. Baggy and big with sleeves that fanned out as I opened my arms. Was it cool? Or contrived? Just then Becca came up from behind me in the blue jumpsuit, pursing her lips like RuPaul. "Ew," she said, gesturing to the caftan.

I tried on a few more dresses. By this point Mom was reading a book of H.D. poems and chomping on trail mix. After trying on ten dresses in total, I was ready to call it a day. Becca, on the other hand, convinced Mom to buy her the jumpsuit, which she wore to dinner that night.

While we freshened up at Mom's hotel, I emailed a few friends and relatives with two pics: one of me in the straitjacket, one of me in the caftan:

Dear sisters and ladies:

i went wedding dress shopping today and found two dresses. am torn. one of them is very traditional (think grace kelly), and the other is a wild muumuu (very, as my mom said, with a horrified expression, janis joplin meets missus roper). i like the missus roper one, but am worried it's unflattering and weird. please take a look and tell me what you think. also, picture it lined, without a slip underneath it, and a good bra to show off the boobs. the grace kelly is totally traditional, but not sure if it's my style.

xox Molly

My aunt Joyce replied:

Who is Mrs. Roper?

By Monday morning, I was back at work staring at my computer, scrolling through wedding dress websites behind my boss's back. Everything looked ugly. Then, one day a few weeks later, I wandered into a fancy store after work. There it was. A drapey, red-and-pink-petal-splotched bustier gown with an ethereal peplum, ruched bust, and a train. I was romantic and cool, like a virginal princess who'd wandered off the beaten path and rolled around in a field of wild raspberry bushes. Done.

The dress cost . . . a lot. More money than I'd ever spent in a single transaction. I left the store in a state of ecstasy, the garment bag under my arm. Then I hung it in the back of my closet for the next eight months. Finally, a few weeks before the wedding, I scheduled an appointment with a seamstress in Manhattan and arranged for her to meet me at my friend's apartment in the East Village. (I lived in Brooklyn.) The seamstress started pinning and I started freaking out. Instead of seeing a lithe bohemian bride before me in the mirror, I saw an obese moose. What kind of tacky hobo would wear such a monstrosity to her own wedding? A demon appeared on my shoulder and announced in my ear, "Why can't you just be normal?" I tore the dress off and fled into the streets bawling.

The next day I put it for sale on eBay. A socialite from Boston swooped it up within the week. The day her payment hit my account, I returned to the downtown showroom on my lunch break and purchased, off the rack, a strapless corset dress with frilly skirt. Over the next few weeks I drank green juice, got colonics, and hoped to become the kind of woman the dress was made for: an easygoing gal who paid all her bills on time and loved pinot and had never experienced deep existential pain. Anyway. I wore the dress on my wedding day. Got my hair done, not my makeup, threw a wrap over the whole thing. The wedding was in an industrial warehouse with huge beamed ceilings and floor-to-ceiling windows. But the floor was filthy. By the time I'd walked down the aisle, the hem of my gown was stained black with dirt. I can't lie; that was kind of my favorite part of the whole look.

# LET'S TALK SHOP

Shopping for your wedding dress is a loaded experience for a million reasons. You're dropping a lot of money, you've enlisted a motley crew of friends to go shopping with, you're forced to confront all your body image issues, the list goes on and on. Wasn't it just yesterday that you were a fun-loving girl having sex with her boyfriend on a dirty futon without a care in the world? Now, suddenly, you're a bride-to-be with a bright future. Soon you will own an expensive waffle maker! You will have three children and a Subaru! You'll glide down the aisle doing the papal wave, poreless and perfect with bleached smile and anus.

Whenever anyone sees my wedding photos the first thing they say is, "Wow, that looks nothing like you," and they're right. If I were to get married now, I'd do it differently. I'd wear a cool hippie dress, dab on some liquid blush, and call it a day. But back then, I went all out: ringlets, the corset and ruffles. It was not at all my vibe but I didn't know there was any other way to do it.

You want to look amazing on your wedding day. You want your hot exboyfriend who dumped you to see your pics on FB and start masturbating and crying. You want that girl who made fun of you at JV basketball practice to follow, in real time, your wedding hashtag on Insta and think, *Wow, she made something of herself.* You want your guests to see you as a peaceful swan who's never had food stuck in her teeth or a bad gas.

Here's the truth: A wedding dress is just a dress. It's not some mystical garment that's going to transform you into the love child of June Cleaver and Gisele. Let's say it again: It's just a dress. Try not to stress too much about it—and don't wear something that's not your vibe. Your dress doesn't have to be frilly. It doesn't have to cinch your waist. It doesn't have to be expensive. It doesn't even have to be a dress.

## CHERCHEZ LA DRESS

If you've spent any of the last ten years watching Kate Hudson movies, you might think that wedding-dress shopping is a dizzying haze of cupcakes, champagne, and flamboyant salesmen with fluffy hair. Not the case. Wedding-dress shopping is annoying and exhausting. Taking the time to find something that you love—whether it's a husband or a dress—is a really messy, nonlinear process. Even if

THE FARRAH

you are a completely organized, type A, Excel spreadsheet kind of gal, finding your dream dress defies all kinds of research and strategy. Ultimately, the decision comes down to your gut. Shopping for your dress is an action; choosing it is a feeling.

Reserve two Saturdays of one month to shop, shop, shop. Take one Saturday to do the whole shebang with your #squad of in-laws, friends, cousins, Mom, etc. This is the time to be silly, to leave your ego at the door, to try on every style of dress. You are not going to buy your dress today. This is research. This is your time to swipe left and keep playing. Watch your blood sugar and pace yourself; the process requires endurance. Bring string cheese and almonds. Designate one friend to take a picture of you in each dress. Even if it's annoying, make sure she gets the pic! Multiple angles are important. Have her take a video of you walking in the ones you like, so you can get a sense of how the fabric moves on your body. After a few weeks off, take another Saturday to revisit your favorites. Now that you know what you like and what you hate, the day should go smoothly. This is the time to be discerning. Ask the salesperson how long it will take for your dress to be made and what their alterations policy is. If you're getting married in the summer, think about how breathable the fabric is. If you're getting married in the winter, consider whether or not you will need a cover-up.

If this whole thing is making your head spin and you absolutely hate "foot shopping" (as our Vintage Specialist Paula calls it), you can order it all online and do a fashion show in front of your full-length closet mirror. Just be sure to check the store's return policy!

## BEFORE SAYING I DO, YOU SOMETIMES JUST HAVE TO SAY "I DON'T."

**Don't** feel like you have to wear white.

**Don't** think you have to buy something expensive. There are plenty of gorgeous vintage dresses to be had for way cheap.

**Don't** get pressured into wearing a relative's dress if you don't want to. Just 'cause it has sentimental value doesn't mean you have to sacrifice your personal style and hate how you look.

**Don't** let some pushy saleslady tell you that you have to order your dress today because *it's gonna take ten months to make.* It's usually BS.

**Don't** buy a dress that you think will look great when you "lose twenty pounds." Buy a dress for the body you have now.

# ALL DRESSED OUT

I've been taking appointments at Stone Fox Bride for over five years now and let me tell you, it's not always pretty. Asking a bunch of women to congregate in one place in your honor sounds great on paper, but in reality it can be a bit of a shit-show. Family members get teary, mothers-in-law get ornery, friends get sloppy on champagne, and there's always that cold cousin checking her phone every four seconds.

In my experience, the most productive appointments are with the women who come in solo. They've done their research, they know what they want, they choose their dress. Easier said than done, though. Most brides end up shopping with the obligatory mix of family and friends. My advice? Only invite people who you know will give you good vibes, no one bitter about a recent breakup or insanely insecure or brutally honest to a fault. If you have to do the whole group thing, then do it with at least one person who really gets you and your style. Then do it again a week later all by your lonesome. Chances are, if you try on a dress, leave it on for more than three minutes, then spend the week thinking about it, it's the one.

# STYLE STORIES FROM FOXES WE HEART

## Stylist Kate Young on Textures, True White, and Total Effortlessness

**On Getting Started:** "Look at pics of yourself in a dress that you love, then figure out what silhouette you feel good in. If you have full hips and a small waist, wear something that's tight on top and full on the bottom. If you're very skinny, a column shape will work well on you. Be realistic. Don't pull a picture of Sofia Vergara if you're shaped like a string bean—it won't look the same on you."

**On Color:** "True white is pretty unflattering on most people. Blush, ivory, or champagne are better options. Hold fabric swatches up to your face and see what works with your skin tone."

**On Shoes and Jewelry:** "I like a shoe with an ankle strap. It's more comfortable and will make your legs look more delicate and thin. When it comes to colors, champagne, silver, or gold are always good options. Sometimes you can pull off a crystal shoe—something in a pale, pale shade of blue or pink. I don't love white shoes, and I think a bright-colored shoe is often a bad idea. At my wedding, I wore huge platforms because I'm massively shorter than my husband. I didn't want to look like his daughter when I was standing next to him. When it comes to jewelry, delicate and classic is the way to go. No big chandelier earrings, no bangles on your upper arms. And don't wear a necklace on your head with a thing dangling down between your eyebrows."

**On Mixing and Matching:** "My general rule is to always work with three textures. For example: wear a crocodile or beaded bag with a silk dress. Avoid having everything match."

**On What She Wore on Her Wedding Day:** "My dress was custom made and loosely based on a tattered dress I found in a Paris flea market. It was totally effortless and fancy and romantic. I love looking like you ran in from the beach and threw on a sparkly dress with sand still in your hair. It's all about ease."

## Fanny Gentle on Combat Boots, Crown Braids, and Hating Big Dresses

**On Her Everyday Style:** "I rode horses when I was a kid—in my free time I used to clean out horse stalls. I was definitely not a girly girl. Dressing up meant wearing combat boots with a tight dress. I've tried out a lot of styles. I had a sixties look for a while and I cut my hair short and dyed it brown. At one point I worked at Urban Outfitters and had a mohawk. Now I'm into looking like an old lady. I wear big shirts or caftans with flat shoes. I'm connected to my grandmother in a weird cosmic way. She had a very unique, interesting style. She really knew herself."

**On Choosing Her Outfit:** "A few weeks before my wedding, I saw these

white dungarees hanging on the rack at the Steven Alan store. I bought them in the spur of the moment. In the back of my head, I thought: *Maybe I'll get married in this.* I knew I wouldn't feel comfortable in a big dress. It's not me at all. I wanted to look pretty my way. I channeled a sort of prairie vibe with a punk edge."

**On Braids and Black Eyeliner:** "I braided my hair that morning and stuck my favorite flowers (anemones) into the braids. Then I put on men's shoes, wore a silver vintage ring with a golden ore stone and a gold bracelet that my mom gave me. My makeup was black cat-eyes and red lipstick."

## Stone Fox Molly Fishkin on Bell Sleeves, BFFs Mary-Kate and Ashley, and Tantrums at the Mall

**On Her Everyday Style:** "I've always been into jeans and T-shirts, but I do love clothes. Most of the time I'm in Levi's and a leather jacket. But when I was a little girl, Stevie Nicks gave me a mini version of the red velvet dress she wore on the cover of her album *The Other Side of the Mirror* (my dad was her manager). It had short velvet sleeves and fifty petticoats underneath. I was so obsessed with it that I wore it every single day for one month. The one time

my mom insisted we wash it I had the biggest tantrum of my life in the Beverly Hills mall. I was six years old."

**On Her Dress:** "I always knew I wanted a long beautiful sleeve of some sort. I love a big sleeve. It reminds me of the seventies, my favorite style era. I'm also insecure about a rash I have on the backs of my arms. I ended up with a custom-made seventies-inspired dress inspired by Margherita Missoni's wedding dress—and I wore it with a simple lace comb veil and nude crocodile Manolos."

**On the Olsens:** "Mary-Kate and Ashley Olsen have been my best friends since seventh grade. We've always joked throughout the years—anytime I started dating a guy—that they would make my wedding dress. When I called to tell them I got engaged the first thing they said was: 'Let's get started on the dress.' I live in LA and they live in New York so the process was pretty involved. I took four trips to the city, had tons of video chats with them, and reviewed sketches via mail. I made a Pinterest board with all my favorite dresses and the three of us reviewed each one together in detail. At the last fitting I couldn't stop crying. It was just perfect."

# "I DID IT MY WAY"
## Q&A'S WITH SOME OF MY COOLEST CLIENTS

The wedding world is a wild industry, which is one reason I love it so much. There was the time my intern walked over the Williamsburg Bridge the day after Hurricane Sandy to deliver a headpiece to a frantic bride getting married that night. The time I stayed up until dawn to make sure that there were eighteen freshwater pearls hand-sewn to an eighteen-foot veil; the morning that Allison Williams from the cast of *Girls* showed up at my apartment two days after I gave birth and got fitted in our Glenda dress for her TV wedding while I sat on the couch in my hospital gown nursing my tiny shrieking baby and wearing a monster-sized Maxi Pad. Making sure all of our brides walk down the aisle in style is a crazy challenge, but I live to make lovely ladies feel foxy. I invited some of my favorites back to the showroom to try on their wedding dresses . . . and got them all dolled up in hair and makeup to relive their white gown moment. Check out their stories that follow.

**FRANCESCA CHOY-KEE**
WORE OUR SILK-DYED AIMEE FLORAL HALO

FRANCESCA CHOY-KEE is an actress and event designer, who married her husband, Matthew, in the backyard of Frankies Spuntino in Brooklyn wearing an SFB veil, silk flower crown, a vintage Edwardian-style dress for pre-wedding photos, and a chic column gown for the ceremony. "After it was over," she says, "our guests lined the entryway to the garden, holding candles, and sent Matt and I on our way."

**On Her Everyday Style:** "Embroidered, romantic, classical, worn at the hem. My grandmother's vintage pocket watch around my neck paired with a vintage Mexican peasant dress I stole from my mom's closet and never returned. I also love my Vans and my wedding rings."

**On Her Biggest Fashion Fail:** "It happened in eighth grade and involved Steve Urkel–style glasses, braces that wouldn't quit, and Princess Leia buns."

**On Choosing Her Wedding Dress:** "I wanted to feel like what I was wearing was an extension of myself rather than a costume. I miraculously found the dress that struck that balance perfectly. Because of a limited budget, I knew

I couldn't go the traditional route of sourcing my dress so I spent a few months doing copious amounts of image research through Pinterest, eventually stumbling upon my wedding dress. The designer customized the gown to my measurements and shipped it to New York, where I tried it on for the first time at my mother's house. For pre-wedding photos, I wore a gauzy SFB vintage Victorian cotton tunic with a delicately crocheted neckline and hem."

**On Accessories and Other Sundries:** "A nude, lacy bralette and Commando seamless briefs. My grandmother loaned me a pair of floral studs and a bangle, both made of 24-karat Guyanese gold. My shoes were these sweet little numbers that imitated laser-cut lace and the heels were gilded in flashes of gold. My clutch was cobalt blue and stuffed with tons of tissues for tears."

**On Putting Her Wedding Dress Back On:** "It felt like a magic cloak . . . I felt strong, beautiful, and deeply myself but even more so because wearing it made me so grateful for the year of marriage I've shared with Matt since I last had it on."

**JENNY SEDLIS**
WORE AN SFB SECOND LIFE BLUSH LACE DRESS
AND RAW-EDGE SILK CHIFFON VEIL

JENNY SEDLIS, executive director of StudentsFirstNY, married her husband, Ben, in Grasmere Farm in Rhinebeck, New York, wearing a raw-edged silk chiffon veil with a fresh flower crown and an SFB vintage pink lace 1930s bias dress. "It felt like the hottest day of the decade," she says, "and after the party, all hot and sweaty, the entire wedding party drove to a nearby lake and went swimming until dawn."

**On Her Everyday Style:** "Monday through Friday is all business. On weekends I wear whatever is relaxed and flowy. My favorite outfit is my Thai fisherman pants, a pair of clogs, and a T-shirt."

**On Her Biggest Fashion Fail:** "At a college Halloween party, my costume was a bubble bath. I blew up all these little white balloons and pinned them to myself. I had on Plexiglass heels that made me six feet tall and a curly white wig that added a few more inches. Some guy came up with a pin and popped all my balloons. For the rest of the night, people asked if I was a drag queen and if the deflated balloons were condoms."

**On Choosing Her Wedding Dress:** "I saw a photo of a pink

lace Chanel dress from the 1930s and just loved it. I knew I wanted something nontraditional and from the thirties and that photo gave me a clearer idea of what I wanted. But I did the wedding dress circuit and hated everything I tried on. Then SFB sourced a 1930s pink lace dress for me and it was perfection. These days, it lives wadded up in a bag because the lace is too tattered to repair."

**On Accessories and Other Sundries:** "My BFF Paula's mom has an incredible antique jewelry collection. The three of us chose a pair of earrings and a couple bracelets from the thirties that complemented the dress perfectly. My bridesmaids got me blue underwear for my something blue. I didn't think I'd care about it but it was fun to pull together."

**On Putting Her Wedding Dress Back On:** "I adore my dress but the lace is so fragile that I keep it rolled up in the back of my closet! It's almost a hundred years old and who knows how long it will last. I loved taking the dress out for a spin and seeing that it still has some life left in it."

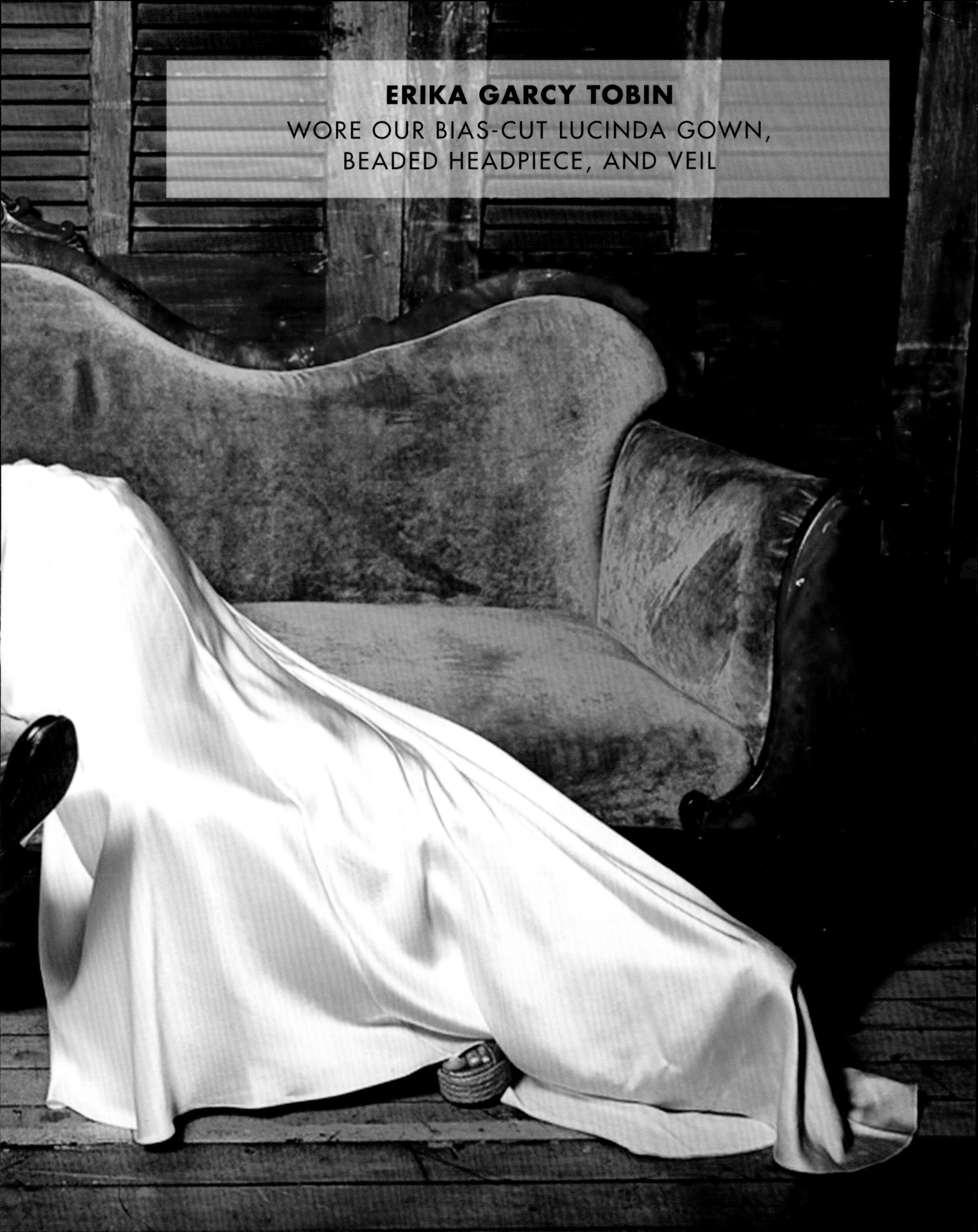

ERIKA GARCY TOBIN
WORE OUR BIAS-CUT LUCINDA GOWN,
BEADED HEADPIECE, AND VEIL

ERIKA GARCY TOBIN is a visual arts teacher who married her husband, Andrew, at the Metropolitan Building in Long Island City wearing an SFB bias-cut Lucinda dress, and lace-trimmed veil with our Tatia halo. "After the wedding," she says, "we ended up at an old classic NYC diner in midtown sharing a meal of mozzarella sticks, chicken fingers, and milkshakes."

**On Her Everyday Style:** "If I could wear one outfit for the rest of my life, it would be sweatpants, a T-shirt, and no bra. When I was a little girl I fantasized about getting married zero times."

**On Her Biggest Fashion Fail:** "Hmm, where to start? My twenties were sprinkled with bad fashion mistakes so it's difficult to pinpoint my biggest blunder. Tube tops, for sure. Tube tops look bad on nine out of ten people and are really just a piece of cheap stretchy fabric that you wear when you want to go out for the night and not come back until sometime the next afternoon."

**Her Advice for Brides-to-Be:** "You worked hard to choose those canapés, skewers, and mini sliders, so enjoy your own wedding cuisine! Ask your coordinator or a friend to put aside a plate for you and your groom to enjoy peacefully during cocktail hour. Andrew and I privately feasted on appetizers and a bottle of bourbon before joining our guests for the festivities. That quiet moment in between the ceremony and the reception was precious."

**On Accessories and Other Sundries:** "Small studs I picked out with my mom and a gorgeous bracelet that my husband's parents gave me. My mom lent me her wedding ring for the ceremony. Under the dress? Nada."

**On Putting Her Wedding Dress Back On:** "I felt silly, like I was a child playing dress-up, nostalgic for the best day of my life, and relieved it still fit."

**SAMANTHA CRABTREE**
WORE OUR BELL-SLEEVED VALENTINA DRESS THAT WE
DYED OMBRÉ GOLD IN MY BATHTUB!

SAMANTHA CRABTREE is a freelance filmmaker and video editor who got married at the Liberty Warehouse in Red Hook, Brooklyn, wearing a gold-ombré SFB bell-sleeve Glenda dress. "It was over 90 degrees that day," she says, "so the girls and I were getting dressed without AC all day. They never got the power up and running, but it was still easily the most fun day of my life."

**On Her Everyday Style:** "The secret love child of Anita Pallenberg and Sun Ra. If I had to wear one thing for the rest of my life, it would be my vintage Mexican blue Josefa dress from the 1970s. It has all kinds of cosmological patchwork all over it. Confidence comes from within, but that dress helps me invoke my most regal self."

**On Her Biggest Fashion Fail:** "I try to steer clear of style-shaming, but I do feel pretty weird about the factory made 'punk' sweater from St. Marks Place that I used to wear a lot in early high school. It had a pre-sewn Dead Boys patch on it."

**On Choosing Her Wedding Dress:** "I started off picturing something like Bianca Jagger's tux, or Yoko Ono's mod mini-dress. The direction I ended up going in was so much more my style. I think I was channeling a combination of Mimi Baez Farina at her Big Sur wedding, and all the ladies from The Source Family. I had an eleventh-hour panic moment after I bought the dress and tried to cancel it, but now I don't know what I was thinking. In the end it was incredible."

**Her Husband's Take:** "My parents INSISTED that I not show the dress to my husband before the wedding, so I didn't but I described it pretty well. We are both highly aesthetic people. His tux was really traditional, but he wore a beautiful gold embroidered tie from Ethiopia."

**Her Advice for Brides-to-Be:** "Well, sample sizes are so friggin' small, so it can be hard for some of us. There were a few dresses that I saw in look books that looked great on the waify model, but when I tried them on I could tell they weren't going to work for my body, even in a size that 'fit.' After a few tries I figured out what cuts I felt best in, and then I wasn't as hard on myself. Try to go in with a sense of what silhouettes make you feel sexy and confident. Magic happens after self-acceptance."

**On Accessories and Other Sundries:** "A nude thong, nip cups, blue nails, silk SFB crown. I borrowed a purse from my mom, and two of my necklaces were old. One necklace had belonged to my husband's grandma."

**On Putting Her Wedding Dress Back On:** "It was pretty funny . . . and it also felt like the end of the whole wedding chapter."

**SUSANNAH CAHALAN**
WORE OUR CUSTOM HONOR SILK FAILLE TOP AND
FULL SKIRT WITH POCKETS

SUSANNAH CAHALAN—the author of *New York Times* bestseller *Brain on Fire*—married her husband, Stephen, at the Dreamland Theater in downtown Nantucket wearing an SFB blusher veil, silk flower crown, and Honor for Stone Fox Bride Astrid skirt and top. "Our ceremony was out on the terrace," she says, "and the day was just plain perfect. It was the last real summer day of the year. We watched the ships go in and out of the harbor as we said our wedding vows."

**On Her Everyday Style:** "Sloppy chic with a bold red lip. If I could wear one outfit for the rest of my life it would be a black sheath dress with sandals."

**On Her Biggest Fashion Fail:** "I have no idea how to iron clothes! It's pathetic."

**On Shopping for a Wedding Dress:** "I was going for 'Brigitte Bardot at the beach.' I love the idea of casual sexiness, lounging beachside and looking fabulous without trying too hard. I'm a little obsessed with Candice Bergen after reading her memoir, *A Fine Romance*. Her wedding to director Louis Malle was just spectacular. She's gorgeous in her long-sleeved gown with her hair all messy and lovely and he's just so in love with her."

**Her Advice for Brides-to-Be:** "As cheesy as it sounds, when you find the dress you truly love, you will know it. Whenever I'm about to purchase a big-ticket clothing item, I always give myself a night to think it over. If you're still lusting over that wedding dress after a few days—if you can't get the damn thing out of your mind—you know you have the right dress."

**On Accessories and Other Sundries:** "I'm very superstitious, so my rings on my left middle finger—a black hematite surrounded by gold—needed to stay put. I wore pearl earrings that my husband gave me for Valentine's Day and rows of freshwater pearl bracelets flanked by garnets gifted to me by my stepmother. Under the dress I wore silky white underwear and a super cute strapless bra."

**On Putting Her Wedding Dress Back On:** "I am so grateful to have lived another day in that dress with all the makeup and the accessories—even the frilly underwear. The experience of dressing up for the shoot was all frothy fun without the gravity of the big day."

**KIM HEYRMAN**

SHE PURCHASED THIS DRESS OFF THE RACK
ONE WEEK BEFORE HER WEDDING.

Model KIM HEYRMAN married her husband, Cody, in September 2013 on Shelter Island, New York, in an SFB silk chiffon bustier dress that she bought off the rack one week before her wedding. "We walked out with the musicians to this beautiful clearing in the woods where all these crazy purple and yellow wildflowers were in bloom," she says.

**On Her Everyday Style:** "If I had to wear one outfit for the rest of my life it would be soft jogging pants, an old sweatshirt, and a nice Prada bag. Plus, good makeup and hair."

**On Shopping for a Wedding Dress:** "I really don't have a style icon. I just wanted to feel confident and feminine and a bit rock and roll."

**On Her Biggest Fashion Fail:** "When I was in middle school I loved to style my hair like Kelly from *Beverly Hills, 90210.* It was huge in Belgium back then."

**On Accessories and Other Sundries:** "I had some antique earrings and a bracelet that I got as a gift from a very dear friend with amazing taste, a Spanx corset thingy, boob stickers, and comfy undies."

**On Putting Her Wedding Dress Back On:** "I couldn't wait to take it off and get back into jeans and sneakers."

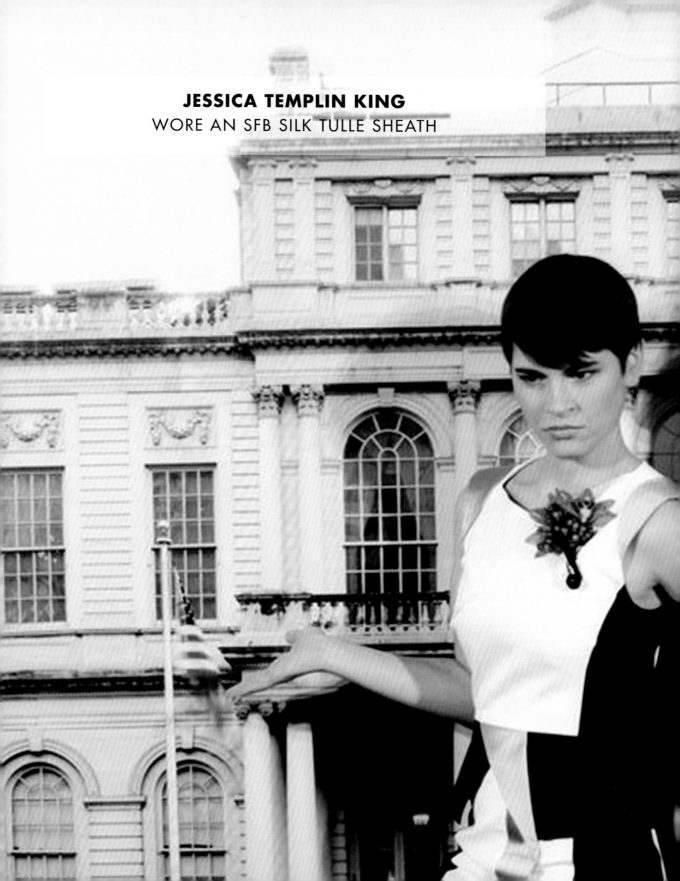

**JESSICA TEMPLIN KING**
WORE AN SFB SILK TULLE SHEATH

Prop stylist JESSICA TEMPLIN KING married her wife, Kaki, at City Hall wearing an SFB silk tulle sheath dress with pearl buttons and a scalloped hem. "After the ceremony," she says, "we went to the High Line and fed each other hot dogs, then had our first dance to a jazz quartet busking in the park."

**On Her Everyday Style:** "I let the big red beach hair lead the way. And my all-time favorite outfit is a slouchy sweater, jeans, boots, and sunglasses. Always sunglasses."

**On Her Biggest Fashion Fail:** "I own a pair of shearling lined Crocs."

**On Finding Her Wedding Dress:** "I knew I wanted sleeves and a deep neckline. Sort of a bohemian Bianca Jagger look. Most bridal gowns out there are so cookie cutter. I wanted to show off my tattoos and be comfortable in a boho meets rocker kind of way. I knew my dress was the one right away: sleeves that showed my tattoos, a deep neckline, full length, beautiful, and comfortable. It was perfect. It now lives in my closet, but I want to have a fun colored slip made for it and wear it for my five-year anniversary."

**On Accessories and Other Sundries:** "Old was my mother's clutch, new was the headpiece, borrowed was my mother's necklace, blue was the hairpin from my sister. I wore a custom slip since the dress was sheer, no bra, and nude underwear. Later I took off the slip and wore a black lacy bra and underwear for (private) pictures."

**On Putting Her Wedding Dress Back On:** "Honestly I was mostly grateful I fit into it . . . three years and one baby later."

**IVY ELROD**
WORE AN ELECTRIC FEATHERS BELTED RUFFLE CAFTAN

IVY ELROD IS a dancer and the owner of a cool Nashville design store called Wilder. She got married in Washington Square Park in July, then rode in a rickshaw to Chinatown for an all-night celebration. She wore an Electric Feathers ruffle caftan dress and a silk SFB veil. "It was 105 degrees," she says. "I was six months pregnant. By far the hottest and coolest day of my life."

**On Her Everyday Style:** "Loose but tight. A hat never hurts."

**On Her Biggest Fashion Fail:** "Platforms under flares creating the dreaded elephant foot."

**On Being a Pregnant Bride:** "I wasn't interested in highlighting my baby bump; not because I wanted to pass as a non-pregnant person (which wasn't even remotely possible) but I felt like my wedding day was about Josh and me. Our son would be starring in most of our days soon enough. Still, my skin looked great. It was summer and I had that whole flushed pregnant bride thing happening. That was a nice bonus."

**On Finding Her Wedding Dress:** "I bought a dress at a big department store in a moment of pregnancy confusion. I was on the road at the time and only in New York for a minute for my sixteen-week pregnancy checkup. The lady there dug out the twenty-six-week fake pregnant belly that they keep in the closet for pregnant brides and then basically looked away while I tried to make something work. I bought the dress that looked the least stupid and regretted it immediately. So I sold it on eBay—then got my dress and veil from SFB!"

**Her Advice for Brides-to-Be:** "Hmm . . . go with your gut. In my case, my pregnancy gut. If

the people around you don't seem genuine or helpful, move on."

**On Accessories and Other Sundries:** "Custom veil from SFB and a flower crown for the reception. Kathryn Bentley earrings that I still wear regularly. Louboutin sky-high heels because I was pregnant, not dead. I borrowed a bangle from my sis and wore some blue underwear, I think."

**On Putting Her Wedding Dress Back On:** "It felt chaotic, magical, and plebeian . . . just like my real life."

# BRIDAL ICONS THROUGH THE AGES

FROM MINIMALIST CHIC TO MAXIMALIST BOHEMIAN,
CHECK OUT FIVE STONE FOX BRIDES WHO CONTINUE TO
INSPIRE US WITH THEIR STYLE AND SWAGGER.

**Yoko Ono:** It was 1969, baby, and Yoko married John in Gibraltar wearing a mod white minidress, kneesocks, and a big white sunhat. Bushy hair + big black sunglasses = best accessories ever. Only a rock star's wife could pull this shit off.

**Bianca Jagger:** Even though she famously said, "My marriage ended on my wedding day," the white YSL Le Smoking jacket and wide-brimmed hat that Bianca Jagger wore for her 1971 Saint Tropez nuptials to Mick Jagger live on in perpetuity. If I only had a dime for every time someone said the phrase "I want to be a Bianca Jagger bride . . ."

**Kate Moss:** John Galliano started dreaming up Kate Moss's wedding gown while he was still in rehab—and upon their first in-person meeting, began pulling out "bags full of bits, and pulled tulle and sequins and veils and flowers," according to Miss Moss. The result was a Gatsby-esque bias slip dress embellished with sequins, gold beading, embroidery, and rhinestones worn with a twenty-foot Juliet cap veil and Manolos. Galliano, who, at the time, was on trial in Paris for the anti-Semitic remarks he made that led him to lose his job at Dior, got a standing ovation when Kate's father, Peter, thanked him for "the beautiful dress" during the speeches. Oy vey.

**Margherita Missoni:** Margherita Missoni turned to her friend Giambattista Valli to design her asymmetrical, voluminous sleeved gown for her 2012 Italian church wedding to racecar driver Eugenio Amos. The dress was made with Missoni silk and organza, covered in a trail of intricate floral appliqués and worn with silver gladiator sandals and a tiara. This is the stuff Bohemian Bride Pinterest boards are made of.

**Solange Knowles:** Beyoncé's baby sis, Solange, married her beau in New Orleans in 2014 and kicked off the festivities by riding in on a white bike with huge natural hair and dewy luminous skin. She wore an ivory jumpsuit-cape combo designed by Stephane Rolland for her grand entrance and then changed into a dress-cape combo designed by Humberto Leon for Kenzo for the ceremony and reception. Her look was chic, sleek, and cool to the max.

# THE LONG AND SHORT OF IT

At the end of the day, wearing a wedding gown might still make you feel totally out of place—kind of like Bridget Jones when she shows up to high tea in that cringey bunny slut suit—and that's fine. Honestly, I'm wary of the bride who doesn't suffer from Impostor Syndrome at some point during the process. The whole thing is inherently weird.

Being a traditional bride was never my cup of tea and I guess it was kind of obvious. Case in point: I married M on Halloween, and when we were walking into our building post-nuptials, we bumped into our neighbor who lived across the hall. She took one long look at me, and, despite the fact I was wearing an ivory bustier and a multi-tiered satin silk gown with a train and holding a huge white box of half-eaten tiered cake, she disappeared into the elevator without uttering a word. She must have thought I was in costume.

# CHAPTER 4

# BEAUTY AND
# THE BEAST

## KEEPING BODY DYSMORPHIA AT BAY
## ON THE BIG DAY

# SKIN DEEP

## HOW I (KIND OF) BID FAREWELL TO
## MY FEAR OF GETTING FAT

UNLESS YOU GREW UP IN a cave without fashion magazines, there's a good chance that at some point in your life, you've hated your body and taken unhealthy measures to try to change the way it looks. The truth is, getting married can turn even the most self-confident lady into a shivering, self-loathing mess. Transitions, even exciting ones, are a perfect petri dish for vulnerability. In the weeks before my wedding, I felt about as secure in my appearance as I did when I was a prepubescent sixth grader with blue braces and one boob.

For some hideous reason, modern-day wedding culture dictates that brides are supposed to look one hundred percent perfect walking down the aisle. Like Miss America–perfect: smiley, shiny, taut, tight, gleaming. God forbid there should be a stretch mark, cellulite dimple, split end, chipped tooth, or cracked cuticle in sight. No wonder so many brides obsess over fad diets.

I'll admit that I've bought into much of this stuff at one point or another.

Blame it on the nineties. I came of age in an insane era when Kate Moss was queen. Homeless and on heroin was the look; drowsy, lead-lidded girls with lank hair and gold hoops in their tits who didn't eat, didn't cry, didn't care. For a good twenty years I struggled with food issues: laxatives, bingeing, purging, the works. So sad. In college I had a "nutritionist" who sold me pyramid schemes of vitamins and delivered deadpan lectures on the high glycemic index of a carrot. Beneath her firm tutelage, I'd record my daily meals in a Moleskine: tiny kale salads, one hundred calories of hard cheese, a single slice of Ezekiel bread. Then I'd have a "cheat day" where I'd pig out on Pringles and pizza. My body image insanity died down around the time I met M, but reared up in the weeks leading up to my wedding. I couldn't get over the fact that everyone was going to be looking at me. I thought I should be on some crazy crash diet, but I wasn't, which stressed me out even more. I guess I was just feeling insecure and vulnerable, trying to control some aspect of the madness.

These days my compulsion to maintain a certain weight is much less crazy

than it used to be. Don't get me wrong, it still flares up every now and then, but way less than before. Sorry to get so Oprah, but the body stuff is a lifelong journey. It comes and goes. Even today, if someone tells me, "You look really healthy," I'll be thinking, *You mean fat?* Try not to use the pressure of your impending marriage as an excuse to emotionally whip yourself. If the mean wedding demon happens to pay you a visit, give him a friendly hello, then tell him to fuck off. My goal is for everyone who reads this book to walk down the aisle feeling like a FOX.

## FEEL FOXY, NOT HUNGRY

**Eat, for Fox Sake:** Diets beget anxiety; anxiety begets bad vibes. Trust me, you don't have to lose weight for your wedding. Do you really want your partner committing to a skinny, withered, unrecognizable version of you? No. Most likely he fell in love and knew he wanted to spend his life with you on some random afternoon when you two were lying naked in bed after really good sex, happy and laughing and probably kind of awkward. Your hair was sticking up, your cheeks were flushed, and you were at your most radiant and comfortable and peaceful. You might have even had a little piece of food stuck in your teeth. Bottom line: You want to look like yourself.

**Good Shape/Bad Shape:** Watch it with the fitness class packs that take place in an air-conditioned room with an instructor on a Bluetooth screaming at you to speed it up. They will most likely turn you into a fidgety, high-stress mess. Better to do something you love in moderation to get in shape: taking long walks, dance classes, bike rides, yoga. Exercising while wearing pajamas in your living room along to Jane Fonda or Richard Simmons is also hilarious.

**Save Face:** I subscribe to the "less is more" philosophy when it comes to most things, makeup included. My wedding beauty regimen was fairly low-maintenance—although I did get my roots done, eyelash extensions, and—truth be told—a spray tan. Looking back at the pics I DEFINITELY could have done without the tan. Whatever you decide, do your damnedest not to overdo it.

**Sweet Dreams:** I know you've heard it before, but getting at least eight hours of sleep a night will do wonders for your skin, vibe, and peace of mind. If you tend toward late nights and/or insomnia, I recommend turning off all devices by eight p.m., taking a warm bath with Epsom salts, and getting into bed with nothing more than a book by ten. The more you sleep, the better you feel. The better you feel, the better you look.

**Rise and Shine:** The morning of your wedding, try to stay away from multiple cups of coffee and sugary white flour things that'll spike your blood sugar. I'm a fan of soft-boiled eggs, oatmeal, berries, tea, and whole-grain toast with almond butter. Take a minute or two to sit silently and gather your thoughts if you can. Beyond the drama, adrenaline, and nerves is the amazing blessing of having found your person. Try to let that sink in on some level.

# BODY POLITICS

OUR PANEL OF STONE FOX EXPERTS WEIGHS IN
ON HOW TO NURTURE YOUR INNER FOXY MAMA
BEFORE YOUR WEDDING DAY.

JOANNA AND HER HUSBAND, CESAR

**The Facialist:** "Two months before the wedding is when you want to pin down what products work best for your skin," says celebrity skin care guru and aesthetician Joanna Vargas. "Stop experimenting. Try to switch to organic and natural products—they assimilate into the body more easily. If you can stop drinking alcohol and avoid caffeine in the weeks leading up to your wedding, that's ideal. These things can make you puffy and give you bags under your eyes. That said, I would have gone psychotic if I didn't have a cappuccino before my wedding, so if you really need one, drink it with gusto. Two weeks before your wedding, start dry brushing your skin before your shower. It's a great ritual that also helps to get all your energy flowing. The morning of your wedding, drink a liter and a half of water to hydrate and get things moving. Spend ten minutes meditating and breathing deeply before you start the day."

Here's Vargas's DIY face mask that's amazing to get your skin glowing. It's calming, exfoliating, and you can whip it up in a few minutes using ingredients in your kitchen:

¼ cup honey
½ cup brown sugar
¼ cup milk
2 tbsp olive oil

Massage the mixture into your skin with a circular motion for several minutes. It will stimulate the lymphatic system, which rids the skin of impurities. Then, leave the mask on for ten minutes. The lactic acid in the milk will assist in smoothing and resurfacing, while the olive oil will act as an anti-inflammatory. Rinse off with tepid water.

**The Trainer:** "Given the stress you'll likely be under, this is not the time to take on your 'Couch-to-5K' fitness program and all-juice diet all at once," says Cadence Dubus, owner of Brooklyn Strength studios. "Hopefully, the person who loves you and wants to marry you already loves you the way you are. Just chill out and try to be consistent with your physical activity and your nutri-

CADENCE DUBUS

tion. Never underestimate the power walk—it burns about as many calories as jogging, no workout clothes needed, just sneakers. Even twenty minutes helps balance hormones and reduces stress. I like to finish it off with some squats or lunges off steps or a park bench—then I use the same steps or bench to do some push-ups. It's a complete cardio and strength workout in a very short time. On the morning of your wedding, take a couple minutes and ask yourself, 'Is there anything I can solve right now, in this moment, that would make me more comfortable or peaceful?' Have breakfast with your mom or your best friend or go for a walk with your dog. Just try to be present and soak up the day."

PATI AND HER HUSBAND, ROBERT

**The Makeup Artist:** "This is not the time to try a new look," says celebrity makeup artist Pati Dubroff, whose clients include Gwyneth Paltrow, Kate Bosworth, and Naomi Watts. "The goal is to look classic and timeless and not overdone. Hire a makeup artist if you want a more polished look in the photographs. When you're interviewing them, look at their previous work to make sure it matches your vibe. Be crystal clear with what your expectations are, what kind of look you want, and how you want your skin to look and feel. I like to look at red carpet photos for inspiration—they're less manipulated and retouched than fashion photos. At the test session take photographs with your phone in different lighting scenarios. If you're not comfortable with the way that the makeup looks, don't be shy to ask the makeup artist to redo it. If you decide to do your own makeup just make sure that you invest in products that are high-quality. Some of my favorites are Laura Mercier primer and Clarins Instant Smooth. Pro concealer is an excellent investment, too. Benefit makes a great waterproof mascara. And be careful with the powder! It will show up in photos that are taken with a flash if it's not blended impeccably well. In terms of lips, the worst is gloppy lip gloss or too-thick lipstick. Go with a red lip if that's your signature look (or if you're doing an outdoor country or beach wedding) but otherwise I'd recommend a light creamy formula with some sheen. A dark smoky eye can work for Saturday evening, but be sure to wear waterproof formula mascara and eyeliner—especially if you're a crier. Blotting papers are great; I love Tatcha papers, as they leave no residue. The morning of your wedding, do some aerobic exercise to put some good, natural color in your cheeks. And these magic wands called Eyecicles are great to massage over your eye and face to relieve puffiness. I keep them in the refrigerator."

**The Hairstylist:** "The most beautiful brides I've seen look like an elevated version of themselves," says hairstylist to the stars Bridget Brager. "Your wedding day probably isn't the time to be experimental and make a huge change. A fun time to be a little crazy style-wise is during the rehearsal dinner—think of it as your red carpet moment where you can try something really high fashion or unexpected. If you color your hair, get it done a week before the ceremony. That leaves you enough time to make adjust-

BRIDGET AND HER HUSBAND, MICHAEL

ments if, God forbid, something goes wrong. Also it usually takes one or two washes before the color settles. Same rule applies for a haircut—if you're going to get one, do it a week before the big day. In terms of wedding hairstyles, one of my favorite updos is the loose halo braid with loose pieces. I also love a beautiful loose braid. And nothing is more chic than a low chignon at the nape of the neck. Hair actually photographs much flatter than it looks in real life, so if you want a beautiful head of voluminous hair in your photos, think about adding in a few extensions. You don't have to go crazy—just a couple singles can make a big difference, especially in the photos. You should obviously do a trial with them first, but on your wedding day, your hairstylist should clip them in after the rest of your hair gets blown out. And a great, natural way to remove product buildup and prepare your hair for your wedding day is to douse it in apple cider vinegar, sit with it for ten minutes, and then wash it out. The only downside is the smell—your hair usually needs a good wash or two to get rid of it. So make sure you do this at least a week before your wedding day."

**The Meditator:** "People have a lot of funny ideas about meditation, usually cobbled together from something they heard on *Oprah,* a random yoga teacher, and a book they picked up two years ago on the spiritual shelf at Barnes & Noble," says awakening coach and meditation teacher Kelly Morris. "Sometimes they think it's only for tree-hugging throwbacks or people who can sit cross-legged or who can't

KELLY MORRIS

cope with the real world. But the truth is, meditation is the number one thing any bride can do to immediately get her act together, calm down, focus on what really matters, and consciously develop her own, unassailable inner compass. Here's one way to do it:

- Sit down in a comfortable position and close your eyes.
- Take a deep breath filling up to the bottom of your feet, allowing your face to relax, becoming like a child: soft, vulnerable, defenseless.
- Allow your awareness to center gently on the feeling of your breath as it moves in and out of your body.

- Open your heart to the universe and give thanks for all the amazing beauty and blessings of this special day.
- Allow the feeling of gratitude to fill up your whole experience.
- Feel yourself going slowly bananas because you have no idea what you are doing—but still stay seated!
- Stay with the feeling you have created for at least three minutes.
- Take one more big breath and head out to your marital destiny.

"Also, the Japanese have a wonderful practice in which they take extended walks in nature alone, inhaling deeply the whole time. The effects are wondrous. Studies show now that the electromagnetic field of a tree, for example, immediately begins impacting you, for the better, draining you of the free radicals (what every product at Sephora promises to do). A steady, grounded freedom is yours for the taking. Develop a consistent practice and experience sovereignty."

# MORNING GLORY

## PRE-WEDDING, THESE STONE FOX BRIDES R&R'D ON THEIR OWN TIME.

**Lauryn Small:** "The morning of my wedding I drove frantically around a tiny island in the Bahamas in a golf cart smoking the remnants of a Cuban cigar while trying to hunt down our wedding DJ (his name was Phat Albert) and our trumpet player. We found the trumpet player passed out drunk under a palm tree and Phat Albert setting up the sound system. Needless to say, I was late to the ceremony."

**Kamara Thomas:** "I get overwhelmed easily, so the morning of my wedding, my maid of honor set up a meditative bridal suite for me filled with candles and pictures of goddesses like White Buffalo, Cat Woman, Rhiannon, and Isis. Only my female friends were allowed to visit, and before the ceremony, nine stood around me in a circle and gave me a little blessing. Then we all got dressed and put on fake eyelashes and burned sage."

**Saga Blaine:** "The morning of my wedding, while recovering from bronchitis, I checked the weather and discovered that a storm was coming in. The ceremony was outdoors and we didn't have a rain plan! I cued up an online yoga video and did chakra flow. In the meantime, my mother-in-law dug a hole next to the trellis where we planned to say our vows and buried a bottle of bourbon there—because according to Southern lore if you bury a bottle of bourbon at the site of the wedding it will keep bad weather away. I guess it worked—the storm never came."

**Gigi Guerra:** "The morning of my wedding, at six months pregnant with twin boys, and wearing a floaty silk tie-dyed tunic, I went to Dunkin' Donuts for chocolate Munchkins. Then I took an Uber to the church, stopping to pick up flowers. I vaguely remember that they were white hydrangeas."

**Torya Blanchard:** "The morning of my wedding, while watching *Sex and the City* reruns, and delirious from lack of sleep, I decided my wedding dress was way too white, so I started dyeing the bottom of it cardinal red using bowls and coffee mugs. I used a hair dryer to get the dress dry, but truth be told it was still damp once we got to the courthouse. Still, I was calm as a Buddha. It came out great."

TORYA DYED THE BOTTOM OF HER DRESS THE MORNING SHE GOT MARRIED.

## SHINE BRIGHT
## FROM INSIDE

Apologies for sounding like a Yogi tea bag, but makeup tips and hair tutorials aside, true beauty comes from serenity and self-love that shines from the inside out. Emotional tranquillity plus tinted foundation/hot yoga/headstands equals a super radiant and relaxed foxy mama. To ensure maximum luminosity, don't be shy about spending your last moments as a single lady solo in your bedroom. Alone with your thoughts, your dreams, and (maybe!) a dildo.

# CHAPTER 5

# MAIDEN'S VOYAGE

## A GUIDE TO ALL THINGS BRIDESMAID

MY BIG SISTER, REBECCA, got engaged five months after I moved to New York City. She immediately anointed me her maid of horror. I mean honor. We were close, but you know how it is with sisters: You hate each other and you love each other. The year was 2000. I was twenty-three, living in the East Village, and I thought I was a real badass. I worked at *YM* magazine and wore smeary eye makeup and slashed Metallica T-shirts. Life had meaning when I made out with a boy or saw a celebrity on the street. While my colleagues worked dutifully at their desks, I stared at the ceiling, dreaming of fame and fortune. In my free time I did karaoke, Jell-O shots, and cocaine.

Becca, three years my senior, was insane, and vicious and beautiful with poreless skin, jet black hair, bright blue eyes, and legs that wouldn't quit. Her yearbook quote? "Most likely to be a spokesperson for Dove soap." By the time I moved to New York, Becca was a Big Apple veteran. The spotless SoHo two-bedroom she shared with her best friend, Martha, was an elegant IKEA catalogue of modular furniture, fresh-pressed frocks, fat-free fruit yogurt, lite beer, apple shampoo, and mint vagina spray. At seven-thirty a.m., with a skinny vanilla latte in hand, Manolos clacking on the pavement, she boarded the 6 train to her uptown office. A burgeoning entertainment publicist, she spent her days on the phone with *Extra TV,* defending Claudia Schiffer (reportedly spotted with a sixth toe in a supermarket parking lot), and placating her candy-addicted boss with Cadbury chocolate. At six-thirty p.m., she rode the train back downtown to the gym and did abs, tush, and treadmill, before meeting up with her crew of Connecticut College friends at some Carrie Bradshaw–like bar. Everything about them was pink, shiny, and sparkly, including their drinks and dresses.

Becca also had a boyfriend, a nice Northwestern grad from a refined Upper East Side family. That spring he proposed to her on a trip to Italy. She floated back home with a Liberace-like gem on her ring finger. I said "Congrats," blinked my eyes, and found myself standing in the dressing room of some wedding store monstrosity, surrounded by layers of crinoline and crinkled taffeta.

BECCA, ME, AND BRIDESMAIDS

There were seven bridesmaids. Seven. Becca chose lavender dresses. I skipped out on most of the dress-shopping thing, and Becca punished me with a hideous high-waisted, JonBenét Ramsey number with a deflated tutu. To get back at her, I spent an entire month's paycheck on hair extensions because I knew it would piss her off. Hair had always been a competitive thing with us, whose was longer, thicker, silkier, better. At Becca's bachelorette party, Martha pulled me aside and begged me to "please reconsider the extensions."

Becca had two showers. The first was hosted by her mother-in-law for the Connecticut crew at some private club uptown and my sister kept reminding me to bring a present. At the time, I was making $25,000 a year and spent much of it on cigs and Brazilian waxes. I bought her a fancy bag of twelve-dollar salt from Williams-Sonoma. Her mother-in-law took one look at it and chucked it quickly into a pile of crumpled wrapping paper. Becca sat beaming in her Herve Leger and Louboutins, surrounded by her nearest and dearest, wearing a paper plate with dangling ribbons.

I hosted the second shower in my East Village studio for a C-list crew of friends and coworkers Becca felt compelled to include out of obligation. I ordered tea sandwiches, had a milkshake bar, and did the hat-ribbon-thing. I took impeccable notes as she opened gifts; "re-ver-si-ble meat tend-er-i-zer, Sur-La-Table," I whispered, imagining hurling the thing toward her face like a tomahawk. I even wore a pink shift with a collar. I really got into character.

The wedding was a blur. I remember midday primping in a stuffy pink hotel suite, the whir of hair dryers, and copious Diet Coke consumption. I remember being very annoyed by a makeup lady with bad breath who descended upon me, vulture-like, and preyed upon my pores with heavy foundation. I sat craving a cigarette, as I watched Becca, so perfect, soaking up the attention like a lizard on a hot rock.

BIG SIS BEC LOOKING LIKE A HOT SLUT BEFORE WALKING DOWN THE AISLE

At the reception, I watched a fashion photographer, and guest of the groom, hit on my model friend who'd recently had two lines in a Tom Cruise movie. She was sleek in a black bias slip. I felt like a giant lavender cupcake in my crinoline. The hours went by and my boyfriend at the time, whom I'd brought as my date, was getting really wasted. I found him smoking cigarettes with the model, and I was furious. I dragged him back to our hotel room and we got in a huge fall-down, screaming fight, which ended when I threw a lamp at his head and banished him into the rainy streets. I fell asleep sobbing wildly and woke up to a pounding headache. False eyelashes were all over the pillow.

Becca and I didn't talk much over the next few years. I'm sure my behavior as her maid of honor had something to do with it. She thought I was sullen and self-involved, that it was obnoxious of me to get those hair extensions, and that I was sort of a bitch. I mean—it's all kind of true.

Looking back now, I realize that I was jealous of my sister. She was in love, she had all these things going for her that I couldn't imagine having for myself, and it was like a gigantic magnifying mirror to all of my insecurities. It's taken us years to work through the drama, but we did it, and now I'm obsessed with her. Plus, all the insane type A stuff that used to drive me crazy? Now I realize how much it's actually helped. Becca has taught me how to write a résumé, give a handjob, and track my ovulation cycle.

And ten years later, she was, of course, my maid of honor. You can bet that the napkins matched the cupcake liners at my shower. When M proposed, she was the first person I told. It was midnight. I texted her our emergency code *MAY-DAY* and she called me right away. When I told her the news, we both started bawling.

Then she said, "You need to send out your save-the-dates on Monday."

# ASK NOT WHAT YOUR BRIDESMAIDS CAN DO FOR YOU . . .

All right, bride-lady. Now's the time to decide: Are you gonna take the plunge and have a wedding party? It's sort of a damned if you do, damned if you don't

scenario. Having bridesmaids is often a recipe for drama, not having them can be a little bit lonely-making. My advice? Do what's right for you. If the thought of having to gather your nearest and dearest for dress shopping and a bachelorette party and a shower makes you reach for your Klonopin, it's totally cool to opt out. If you absolutely adore your bitches and must have them by your side at all times, then this is the time to round up the troops!

Whatever you decide, I'm all for reframing the whole dynamic between the bride and her maids. Instead of demanding that they cater to your every need, use this time as an opportunity to let your ladies know how much you love them and value their friendship. Then, designate one friend to liaise between you and the group. This way, you avoid being blindfolded and led to a hotel room in Atlantic City (unless you want to). Plus you can circumvent the inevitable party planning power struggle and you make things easier on the whole crew. Whatever you decide, here are some tips that will help you navigate this potential landmine with style and grace.

Okay. First things first. Don't do it. Don't have bridesmaids. It's stupid. It's a popularity contest. It will make everyone miserable. You will lose friends, you will make enemies, you will have to manage personalities. You will end up with a whole crazy cast of peeps from all of the different parts of your life and it will inevitably be a total shit-show. You will have to get wasted at the bachelorette party to deal with all the weird vibes. Skip the drama.

Okay, fine. Have bridesmaids. It's kind of nice to gather your main bitches and celebrate the love you have for your partner. Plus, you get gorge pics of everyone in fancy dresses with flowers. Just be sure to choose women who make you feel elevated and happy, who you can be your weirdest, lamest, most neurotic self around.

Be really sensitive to the money stuff. We all have different incomes and are comfortable spending different amounts. When planning bridal party activities, realize that a weekend in Miami with four-star-restaurant reservations might not be feasible for all folks. Bowling and dim sum can also be cool. The idea here is to be inclusive. The last thing you want is for friends to feel bad about themselves.

On that note, you cannot insist that everyone buy a four-hundred-dollar dress. You are basically signing yourself up for your friends to talk behind your back and send emails about how you are an entitled bitch. And unless you're footing the bill, demanding that your bridesmaids with varying body types and coloring wear identical dresses is also a ticking time bomb. Instead, create an inspiration board on Pinterest and share it with everyone. Tell them to pick a dress they love, within your expansive parameters, whether it's a vintage frock, something from a cool boutique, or a find from Etsy. Whatever works for their vibe and budget. Another idea is to have everyone pick a white dress that they can dye in the color of your choice. And your bridesmaids' dresses don't have to match! (Destiny's

Child figured this out in 1999.) You're better off with dresses your friends might actually wear again and will feel their best in.

Don't expect your friends to read your mind. Nothing is worse than a bride—harboring secret resentment for weeks—who suddenly starts screaming and crying hysterically, and runs to the bathroom, dramatically. If, for example, it's important to you that all your bridesmaids arrive on time to various events, then tell them that. If you want them to clean up the bridal suite so that your mom doesn't have to, tell them that, too. Be clear from the get-go about your needs.

Conversely, be realistic when it comes to expectations. If your best friend just had her second kid and has sutures holding her vagina together, she is probably not going to be the most prompt and perky member of your #girlgang. Don't take it personally. If another friend can't make it to your bachelorette weekend because she is graduating from med school, let it go. Major bummer, yes! But it has nothing to do with you.

Do let your bridesmaids play to their strengths. If you have a crazy writer friend who is notoriously disorganized, don't ask her to plan your bachelorette party. Instead, ask if she wouldn't mind reading a poem during the ceremony. Conversely, if you have a friend who hates public speaking but is really good with Excel spreadsheets, have her handle RSVPs and seating arrangements.

Do remember to acknowledge your bridesmaids. Don't underestimate just how far a simple handwritten "thank you for your help and support" can actually go. Take your maid of honor for dinner at a restaurant of her choice with the rule that the topic of your wedding is off limits. And the first time you all convene, give everyone a personalized Bridesmaid Survival Kit. Some essentials to choose from:

- SFB "Fuck Weddings" linen tote (shameless plug here)
- A sage bundle smudge stick
- Candy
- A good book (Toni Morrison, Sylvia Plath, or Judy Blume will do)
- Moroccan slippers

ONE OF THE SFB BRIDESMAIDS SURVIVAL KITS

- Rosewater face mist
- Dry shampoo
- Lavender essential oil
- Healing crystals
- Blush/lipstick/lip gloss

# KEEP CALM AND LET YOUR BRIDESMAIDS CARRY ON

ALL TRESPASSING BRIDES WHO READ THIS NEXT SECTION WILL BE SUBJECT TO A LAP DANCE BY A MALE STRIPPER WITH WAXED BALLS AND A WILLIE NELSON WIG. THE FOLLOWING SECTION IS FOR THE BRIDAL PARTY ONLY.

All right, so your BFF is getting hitched. Stop hyperventilating. The bachelorette party doesn't have to involve white limos, Pin the Penis on the Donkey, and an insufferable Vegas weekend with ten women who don't know one another. Who says that getting a bride and her best bunch of gals up in a room together has to turn into a spring-breaker-like bacchanalia featuring edible underwear, Jell-O shots, and dick lollipops?

Good wholesome fun, girls. That's what I'm all about. Some of my best ever girl-bonding moments were in middle school—over pints of ice cream, Patrick Swayze movies, and sweatpants. There was giggling galore, tons of gossip, good food, and a cozy vibe that was all about being unself-conscious and in the moment. Nothing beats a laid-back hang with your besties.

As you, dear bridesmaid, prepare to sherpa your friend into the next phase of her adult life, why not give yourself permission to go back in time? Pull on your yoga pants, grab a pillow, and embrace your inner seventh-grade dork. Cool girls in slutty black dresses need not apply. Here are some DIY bachelorette ideas for the blushing prepubescent in all of us.

## DYE JOB

Scrunch up damp white silk scarves (buy in bulk on Etsy) or hankies in a tin or colander, and cover fabric completely with a layer of crushed ice. Sprinkle various colors of DRY dye on top until the ice is mostly melted (okay to use a hair dryer to accelerate the melting). Dump the remaining ice and water, and run under cold water until it runs clear. Et voilà!

# CUPCAKE BAR

Remember when you would make cupcakes from a box and eat half the batter after school? Same principle applies here. Bake a bunch of chocolate and vanilla cupcakes (from scratch or from a Betty Crocker mix). Have your foodie friend bring a bunch of piping bags and a huge bowl of homemade buttercream frosting. Then go to town with food coloring and sprinkles.

## SLEEPOVER, GROWN-UP STYLE

Book a suite at a hotel, order room service, watch pay-per-view, take bubble baths, eat candy, drink champagne, tell penis jokes, play board games, pass out before midnight.

## HOST A SPIRITUAL SOIREE

Google a local psychic, stick-and-poke tattoo artist, moon goddess, tarot reader, or a blow job specialist. Invite the guru over and have everyone's chakras aligned with crystals, their auras read, or fellatio skills honed. It's never too late to learn.

Write Val a secret message that she can carry with her into her married life and tell her why you love her! We will mail it out in the weeks before the wedding

## P.S., I LOVE YOU

Create a letter writing station. Address a bunch of envelopes to the bride, decorate them with heart stickers, and ask everyone to write her a love note. Have the maid of honor mail out one a day the month before her wedding.

## HAVE FUN WITH FLOWERS

Buy flowers, floral wire, wire cutters, and ribbon. Google "DIY flower crowns" and go to town. Sit in the park and kumbaya while you're at it. Flower bashing is another great way to bond and release pre-wedding aggression. Lay out a ton of colorful blooms on some canvas totes on a flat wooden surface, cover with wax paper, and pound the shit out of them with hammers. Both the experience and the result are super psychedelic.

## MAKE YOUR OWN DRINKS

We all love a good artisanal, organic muddled cocktail, but isn't the mustachioed man in suspenders who makes it kind of annoying? (Not to mention that seventeen-dollar price tag.) To customize your own booze, buy some seasonal herbs, seltzer water, alcoholic mixer, edible flowers, and fruit. Think bourbon, rhubarb bitters, blueberries. Or, fuck the fancy stuff, whip out the blender and make piña coladas. Extra maraschino cherries, OBV.

## CHICKS BEFORE DICKS

If you must incorporate a naked man into your bachelorette party bacchanalia, does he have to wear a G-string and be banging his balls against the bride's forehead to 2 Live Crew? Methinks not. Neither does Fleur Childs, founder of The Artful Bachelorette, an innovative events company that organizes bachelorettes, bachelors, birthdays, and get-togethers that center around live figure drawing (read: naked man). The two-hour classes feature champagne, music, and a male model—along with a drawing coach who arrives with sketching pads and pencils. "It's not about being Picasso," says Childs. "Just expect to learn a little and laugh a lot."

# SPEECH THERAPY

## PUBLIC SPEAKING MAKES YOU TONGUE-TIED, BUT AS MAID OF HONOR, YOU HAVE TO GRAB THE MIC. WHAT TO DO? HAVE NO FEAR, SFB IS HERE.

I've sat through some very, very long wedding speeches in my day and let me tell you, it ain't fun. The goal is to make the bride look and feel super special, but not at the expense of alienating other guests. Think of your speech in the same way you would a cover letter—thoughtful, succinct, and personable. It's NOT a private text thread full of mushy, run-on sentences and heart emojis. Keep it direct, under seven minutes, and conspicuously absent of stories involving exes, hookups, or anything remotely embarrassing.

Here is my formula:

The story that comes to mind when I think of _____ is the time that she a) *delicately picked up a baby bird from a fallen nest and placed it out of harm's way* b) *stood outside of prom with a picket sign and pajamas protesting fast fashion and child labor laws in China* c) *stared down the eighth grade playground bully when she mocked my headgear* d)_____ (fill in the blank, you get the idea). In that moment I saw the depths of her a) *compassion* b) *integrity* c) *loyalty* d)_____ *pick an adjective then talk about how deeply it touched you and why.* Then move into the first time that you realized that _____'s partner was more than a casual hookup, like when he a) *stayed up with her all night feeding her saltines after she caught food poisoning on their second date* b) *picked up her grandma Myrtle from her colonoscopy* c) *encouraged her to apply for the Peace Corps in the slums of Liberia for a whole year instead of moving in together* d) _____ *etc., etc.* Then a sincere wish for their future together; may it be full of a) *peace +adventure* b) *security + abundance* c) *prosperity + babies* d)_____ *blah blah blah,* topped off by something along the lines of *no matter where, no matter when, no matter how, I will always be here for you when you need me, etc., etc.*

Now cheers and sit the fuck down.

# STRENGTH IN NUMBERS (OR NOT)

THERE'S NO RIGHT WAY TO HAVE A BRIDAL PARTY.

## Andrea Cashman on Moon Earrings, Marie Antoinette, and Having Eight Bridesmaids

**On Her Bridal Party:** "I chose eight bridesmaids because I have so many incredible women in my life. There was Alexis, who I've known since I was born, a master oenologist who worked on a biodynamic vineyard in New Zealand. She chose all the wine for the wedding. There was Kristina, who I met when I was twelve and wearing a really ugly hat, but she still wanted to be my friend. My friend Simone is an outdoor landscaper, so she did all the floral arrangements. The list goes on. I thought of them as my muses, each bringing her own talent and personality into the mix. I also had two maids of honor—I felt like I needed to honor them both."

**On Their Dresses:** "The inspiration for their dresses was a mixture of the Flower Fairies, Shakespeare's *A Midsummer Night's Dream,* and Marie Antoinette's milkmaid phase. Their dresses were meant to echo the wildflowers at our venue—and also be cool enough so they could be worn on the streets of NYC with boots and jean jackets. I offered to pay for half of each dress, presented my bridesmaids with a bunch of swatches and let them choose whatever color suited them. The dresses also came in a variety of lengths. I didn't want them to be these long, formal, ugly, stressful things."

**On Primping and Prepping:** "The night before the wedding, two of my bridesmaids slept over with their partners. We woke up a little hungover from the rehearsal dinner, and took a swim in the river. It was freezing cold and refreshing. Afterward, we got right to work. It was not a leisurely time! I had everyone arranging flowers and making signs. We didn't stop until two hours before the wedding. Finally, one of my girls was like: 'Go get ready.' I gave them their gifts a few hours before the ceremony—moon and star earrings—because they were each like guiding stars in my life. We all got ready together in this beautiful old

ANDREA WITH HER EIGHT BRIDESMAIDS. RANDOM FACT: WE HAND-DYED EACH ONE OF THOSE DRESSES!

farmhouse. We drank wine and ate cheese while we did our own hair and makeup. There was lingerie and jewelry and rollers flying everywhere. Tons of giggles in the air."

**On the Ceremony:** "My husband and his groomsmen were waiting for us by a river bend near a giant tree. All of the bridesmaids meandered down this huge hill toward them, through a path of wildflowers. Then my mom and dad walked me down the hill. Kristina sang 'Hyberballad' by Björk, Alexis read a passage from *Pippi Longstocking*. There was a moment during our vows when I looked back at the bridal party and saw them all standing there—weeping profusely, these beautiful wildflowers, all at once."

## Johanna Almstead on Hurricane Sandy, Bad Boyfriends, and the Power of the Best Friend Bridesmaid

**On Bridesmaids:** "I was in my mid-thirties when I got married and it felt so silly to ask my friends to buy matching dresses that they didn't want to wear. The whole rigmarole, the organizing and the fighting and the drama . . . I really didn't want to deal. But I knew I didn't want to be alone up there."

**On Choosing Her "Person":** "My BF and I met in statistics class at FIT and have known each other for twenty years. After I was engaged I said to her over drinks, 'You're going to be my person, right?' and she was like: 'Of course!' I couldn't even call her my bridesmaid or maid of honor."

**On the Dress:** "I didn't want to tell her what to wear. We're grown women—she can dress herself. She ended up in an amazing black cocktail dress and Jimmy Choo shoes. Also, she carried a tiny bunch of burgundy calla lilies."

**On the Wedding:** "I wanted a fabulous New York dinner party with amazing food and wine and fun people. It was a few weeks after Hurricane Sandy and we didn't even know if the restaurant was going to have power. The cab dropped us off at the wrong entrance to the restaurant, so she had to carry my dress through the dishwashing station in the kitchen. It was super silky and slippery and had a long train. As we were waiting in the wine cellar for the ceremony, she looked at me and we both welled up. We'd been through it all together: all the bad breakups, all the bad boyfriends, and there we were. After a while she said: 'You got this.' "

### Amy Foote on Lucinda Williams, Homemade Jam, and Not Having Bridesmaids

**On Getting Married:** "Growing up, I never fantasized about marriage or my wedding. Ana was really into the idea of marriage, however, and even though I was totally in love with her and felt 'committed,' I had never been super concerned about it before so I had to do a lot of thinking about what marriage meant to me. I read a few books about the history of marriage, but nothing really clicked until my sister got married. I was really excited about her husband finally becoming a part

of the family and I thought, 'That's what I want!' The wedding took place in Silver City, New Mexico. That's where my wife grew up. It was a great excuse to get all our friends to a beautiful place that means a lot to both of us. The ceremony was up the mountain at the Pinos Altos Opera, a magical opera house from the 1860s that is now fighting decay. Attached is the Buckhorn Saloon, featuring paintings of scantily clad ladies. How could we not pick a place like that?"

**On Choosing to Not Have Bridesmaids:** "I have a friend who's ten years older than me who would always say, 'Once you turn thirty, you have to stop blaming your parents, stop asking your friends to help you move, and you can no longer have bridesmaids at your wedding.' It kind of stuck. Plus, the first time I was a bridesmaid, I didn't realize that there were all these roles and responsibilities and I felt like I failed my friend. I also thought that having bridesmaids promotes this idea of a hierarchy within your friendships, which I didn't like. Having a flock of ladies standing next to me was not something that appealed to me. It felt a little too traditional and patriarchal. I think my friends were probably relieved not to have to buy matching dresses and play a role. In the end, our sisters and friends read and sang during the ceremony as a way to honor our community without all the pressure and expectations. Also, my wife's family members are western libertarian hippie types and they didn't care about the wedding being traditional. We ended up using the ritual parts of the wedding ceremony that rang true for us and discarded the rest, especially the traditional gender-specific stuff. For example, we wanted both of our parents to give us away, so they both walked both of us down the aisle."

**On Random Deets:** "We made 120 jars of homemade pear, ginger, and peach rum jam into the wee hours of the night before. Our wedding was DIY. We did everything but cater it. Our friend Steve James, an amazing blues musician from Austin, played steel guitar, and our friend Mya sang a Lucinda Williams song, 'Like a Rose.' "

*OOO*

# HI, MY NAME IS _____AND I HAVE POST-TRAUMATIC WEDDING PARTY DISORDER

## BRIDESMAID HORROR STORIES FROM THE FRONT LINES*

"The bride asked me and one of our closest friends to be bridesmaids. Then, her husband didn't have enough friends to even out the wedding party, so she retracted the invitation and eliminated our friend as a bridesmaid. Red flag #1. The day of the wedding, she gave out the bridesmaid gifts: chandelier earrings. I didn't get a gift because my ears aren't pierced. After the ceremony, as the bridal party was making their way to the limo, the bride told us that there wasn't enough room for everyone, got inside, and drove off. Some random uncle took me to the pictures in his car and got me a bottle of Burnett's vodka to chug on the way there. Then, we took pictures in the Saint Louis humidity for two hours and I ended up with a yeast infection from sweating under my floor-length dress."

"I was in a serious car accident the week before my wedding, so the wedding sort of felt like I just had to get through it. One of my bridesmaids who knew about the accident, sent me a text the day before the wedding to ask how things were going. I was emotionally spent at that stage, and I gave her the honest answer: *I'm not great, I'm really beat, I'm so upset things happened like this and I won't really be able to enjoy it.* Her response: *Oh no :( I have news!!!!!! James just proposed!!!* The. Day. Before. My. Wedding."

"The bride wanted us all to pick our own dresses in a neutral color. I found a light pink dress I loved. It was asymmetrical with one black strap. The bride objected immediately because of the strap, despite sending lots of dresses for me to consider that had black bows. Not to mention that she let a fellow bridesmaid wear a white lace dress. We got together for a beer and I tried to tell her how her obses-

---

\* Don't be scared. Unless your maid of honor is a Mob wife, this will not happen to you.

sion with every little wedding detail was making me and the other bridesmaids feel. I said she needed to let the color of the strap go. She yelled out in response, 'I'm not having a black strap at my wedding!' She gave me a choice of a couple of different shades of ribbon that I could use to replace the strap and we agreed on a dark purple one (basically black). After all that, she made me wear a glittery cardigan during her ceremony. She also seated me away from the rest of the wedding party at the back of the dining room. I'm now cropped out of her wedding photos."

# BOTTOM LINE:
## STEER CLEAR OF CATFIGHTS

Having a bridal party is bound to get messy at some point, but just remember, when the shit goes down, you're all playing for the same team. Dress swatches, hair and makeup, party favors . . . keep it all in perspective. It's just a wedding! If, at this moment, the chemistry of your bridal party is kind of cunty, close this book immediately, send a "sorry for the bad vibes" group text, and invite them all over to drink beer and watch *Bridesmaids.*

# CHAPTER 6

# BUDS + BLOOMS
## FINDING YOUR INNER FLOWER CHILD

CHOCOLATE COSMOS, crimson gardenias, dark scarlet camellias. In my twenties, I dated a guy named Finn who not only loved flowers but knew all their names. He'd often show up in my foyer holding an opulent bouquet, so large it obscured his face. Down the street from his apartment was a jewel-box of a flower shop, pristine white and glass, and the blossoms they sold were nestled in rice paper, tied with raw twine, and started at twenty dollars a stem. Basically, each bouquet was around two hundred bucks. Not that Finn cared.

We were both regulars at Doma café in the West Village. We avoided eye contact for months before he introduced himself. He had pale eyes and a PhD in philosophy. He lived around the corner in a huge railroad apartment with a working fireplace and a velvet couch. His silver hair was sleek with Brylcreem. One of his proudest possessions was a self-published book of photographs he'd taken of doors. He came from a lot of money and was proudly unemployed. Wounded, lyrical, and tormented, Finn's whole life was a self-produced series of tiny, curated moments, each one more intoxicating than the next.

We were both born around Valentine's Day. We both had older sisters. We'd spend afternoons doing nothing but kissing on this one Bleecker Street park bench. We'd listen to Spanish guitar with the windows open. His favorite quote by Flaubert was "Language is a cracked kettle on which we beat out tunes for bears to dance to, while all the time we long to move the stars to pity." I would nod solemnly when he uttered the passage, but I had no idea what it meant.

Finn was both withholding and high-maintenance. He used to leave the room mid-argument to email his online life coach for advice. He had a Ukrainian heir-

ess ex-wife and a troubled older sister who lived down the street and who once wore a mink stole on the hottest day of July. He also had difficulty maintaining an erection, once accused me of leaving a bruise on his dick, and oftentimes, while we were fooling around, would leap up, cry out "oh god," and launch into the details of his mother's slow gruesome death from cancer for the four hundredth time. The flowers kept coming, though. Violets and sweet peas, hydrangea and jasmine, ranunculus, big as a baby's heart. But we started seeing each other less. Eventually each time he flourished a bouquet I felt secretly crushed by the suspicion that the new flowers would outlast his interest. Guess what? I was right.

THAT'S HOW everything was in my twenties. Nothing lasted. The one ring I wore all the time—a rose gold signet—had a fire opal center stone that was so soft it crumbled in the bath. Every fall I bought the same black suede boots that were destroyed months later by slush and snow. I brought a cat home from the ASPCA and gave her away a few years later when her sneezing started to drive me crazy. And my friends? Pretty, flitty, unreliable. We darted from party to party tangled in each other's tattooed arms, but God forbid we remembered each other's birthdays. If my pre-married life were a flower, it would have been a poppy. Bright red, paper-thin, petals frayed and torn. At some point, the whole lightness-of-being thing started to wear off. What I craved I couldn't get: a warm home, lasting friendships, real love.

As far as flowers go today, M rarely buys them for me. Every now and then he proudly barrels into our building with an armful of carnations, and I'm all: "Babe, you're so sweet!" But let's be honest—a carnation is like the Glade candle of flowers. Presents M has given me over the years include an organic towel, a

reading lamp that's also a necklace, a blue fleece shirt, and a filing cabinet. One time he surprised me with an anniversary weekend in Bermuda, but mostly he's a practical guy: cooks spaghetti, sticks to his word, handy around the house. My mom always says "Love is a verb," and I think she's right.

Depending on the season, I'll always have a pot of something on my kitchen table. Sunflowers, tulips, fresh mint from my patio—mainly just durable blossoms that require minimal energy to maintain. Who knows, maybe down the road I'll grow a wild, world-famous rose garden, or become an eccentric old orchid collector with a long gray braid and tons of cats. I still don't understand what moves the stars to pity, but I do know now where to look for real romance. And it's not inside a vase.

# PUT ON THOSE ROSE-TINTED GLASSES

"I hate flowers. I paint them because they're cheaper than models—and don't move."

—Georgia O'Keeffe

Flowers can be a surprisingly stressful part of the wedding planning process. Though I love beautiful blooms, I can think of no greater hell than trying to memorize the names of all the different kinds of flowers, and the regions they come from. But you don't have to have a PhD in horticulture to take an active role in choosing your wedding flowers. I knew next to nothing about flowers when I got married so I found a random florist through my wedding planner, never even met her and instead just loosely uttered a few things to her on the phone about succulents, loose ferns, pomegranates, and candles. Bad move, and I paid the price for it on my wedding day. My bouquet resembled a college dorm room ficus plant. The tablescapes were dumb and my flower crown was a monstrosity of pipe cleaners and plastic beads. I still wake up in the middle of the night thinking about it.

You know more about flowers than you think you do. Think back on your life so far. Did someone close to you have a garden? What flowers have been given to you at meaningful times? What did they look like? What did they smell like? How long did you keep them? Find inspiration in what you already own. Cull from family photos and pop culture. I have always loved marigolds, for example, because my grandpa Dave sent them to me after I had ear surgery when I was four. What is your favorite flower reference from a movie? I love the scene in *Harold and Maude,* when Ruth Gordon (one of the original Stone Foxes, btw) and Bud Cort are walking through a field of daisies and she says to him: "Look—some are smaller, some are fatter, some grow to the left, some to the right, some even have lost some petals, all kinds of observable differences. You see, Harold, I feel much of the world's sorrow comes from people who are this, and allow themselves to be treated as that . . ." Hello, isn't that the most beautiful thing ever?

*Sixteen Candles* is another film I always go back to for inspiration. The pink-and-blue flower crown Samantha wears to her sister's wedding is very eighties, slightly heinous, but cool because it's Molly Ringwald. And then there are books. When I was a depressive prepubescent in a training bra, my favorite novel ever was *A Summer to Die* by Lois Lowry—about a teenage girl who died of leukemia and whose grave was heaped in goldenrod. Ever since, I've secretly had a goldenrod fetish. (I know my flower references are really dark and weird, sorry.) The point is to find your own mental arsenal of budding inspiration. What perfumes do you like? What color gems are you drawn to? Look at the rugs in your house, open up your closet. Don't just look for floral patterns. Think about textures and colors. Listen to your intuition. What are your favorite songs about flowers? I'm obsessed with "Lilac Wine" by Nina Simone.

# FIND YOUR
# FLORAL VIBE

WE WORKED WITH RAWAN RIHANI
OF AURORA BOTANICA TO CREATE
FIVE ICONIC BOUQUETS.

## If Your Style Icon Is . . . Carolyn Bessette-Kennedy

**Your Flowers Should Be:** Minimal, spare, and all white. Conceptual blooms with strong posture and straight spines: calla lilies, lilies, and lily of the valley. Avoid anything loose, droopy, hippie-ish, or asymmetrical.

**Flower Crown?** Not your thing. But why not tuck a single bloom behind one ear?

**Consider Tying Your Bouquet With:** One gorgeous thin strand of pure white raw silk twine. Or just walk down the aisle holding one beautiful calla lily stem nonchalantly—like an afterthought.

**Table Centerpieces:** Shallow blown-glass bowls of water (to hold floating lilies), classic glass vases with long graceful necks filled with calla lilies.

## If Your Style Icon Is . . . Kate Moss

**Your Flowers Should Be:** Wild, fragrant, and relaxed. Think Juliet roses, peonies, honey clematis, sage, rosemary, mint, strawberry cuttings, fragrant stock flower, lace ferns, citrus, and cherry blossoms. If these flowers were a hairstyle, they would be last night's still-smoky bedhead ringlets, post–Studio 54 bender.

**Flower Crown?** For sure. But no need to overdo it here. Classic and understated: garden spray roses, rabbit ferns, and astilbe.

**Consider Tying Your Bouquet With:** A vintage diamond-encrusted bra strap that once belonged to Josephine Baker.

**Table Centerpieces:** Large, shallow antique cast-iron pots that double as vases. Opulent table garlands of peonies, roses, red grapes, and pomegranate seeds (that leave juicy ruby stains on the tablecloth).

## If Your Style Icon Is . . . Dita Von Teese

**Your Flowers Should Be:** Reminiscent of a boozy, dimly lit nightclub filled with burlesque dancers and whiskey—nothing too flowery, feminine, sweet smelling, and NO PINK! Chocolate cosmos, tobacco flower, mint, valerian root, moon flowers, and dark grapes preferred.

**Flower Crown?** Nope. Think classic wrist corsage made with one black dahlia and a few berries.

**Consider Tying Your Bouquet With:** A distressed, raw brown leather strap that once belonged to a dominatrix.

**Table Centerpieces:** Tobacco flowers, mint and black dahlias in heavy, vintage cemetery vases.

## If Your Style Icon Is . . . Elizabeth Taylor

**Your Flowers Should Be:** Inspired by rubies, emeralds, diamonds, and sapphires. Red roses, delphinium, violets, ruby dahlias, clematis, and white peonies.

**Flower Crown?** Nope. Do a diamond-encrusted tiara adorned with lilacs and lilies instead.

**Consider Tying Your Bouquet With:** A deep red velvet ribbon.

**Table Centerpieces:** None! Do a huge chandelier-like installation hanging above the table dripping in clematis and precious gems.

## If Your Style Icon Is. . . . Frida Kahlo

**Your Flowers Should Be:** Dark peonies, dark poppies, dark roses, crimson garden roses, Juliet roses, burgundy ranunculus, and bleeding hearts. It's also okay to use a sunflower or two, but sparingly. The goal here is moodiness and drama.

**Flower Crown?** A wreath of wild red roses, natch.

**Consider Tying Your Bouquet With:** No bouquets. Think double wrist corsage and ring-to-wrist hand chain made with wild vines and marigolds.

**Table Centerpieces:** The bigger and more unconventional, the better. Think volume, height, and width. Mountains of poppies, dahlias, and dark roses overflowing from hand-spun, hand-painted bloodred clay pots.

## SEED MONEY: WORKING WITH A FLORIST

Are you the type to pop into a new salon and tell a random hairstylist, "I don't care, have your way with me?" Yeah, me neither. Not sure why I thought I could do this with my wedding florist. Being hands-off put me in a position of having zero creative control. I couldn't even complain about it later, because I hadn't offered up any thoughts on what I wanted from the start. Would it have killed me to make a mood board? If you decide to

hire a florist, make sure you participate in some of the decision making—I promise you'll be happier with the outcome if you do some research beforehand. That said, you also don't want to go overboard. If you trust your florist, communicate what you want, then let her do her thing. No micromanaging allowed! We once did flowers for a bride who was so type A that she couldn't stop screaming about the fact that there were only fourteen cherry blossom branches in each vase instead of fifteen. Right before her ceremony started.

# WELCOME TO THE JUNGLE

*Florist Lisa Prystup on Overgrown Arrangements*

**On Choosing Your Florist:** "Take a wide sample—check out as many websites as you can and make a list of florists whose arrangements reflect what you want. It's kind of like applying to college. Pick six that you find interesting—two dream florists, two safety florists, two middle of the road ones. Have a conversation with each, and ask them to present you with an inspiration board detailing their price range and their color schemes. You should also be prepared to send them your own inspirations so you know you're on the same page. All of this

LISA PRYSTUP

should happen before any money is exchanged. Definitely do a lot of research on your end. Keep your communication lines open and be clear about what you want. Also, flowers are expensive—be prepared for that reality."

**On Her Most Memorable Mistake:** "Once, when I was just getting started, I was working with a couple who wanted long eucalyptus garlands hung vertically from the ceiling. It seemed totally doable—only I didn't realize until the day of how high the ceilings were! I ended up having to run out to Home Depot, buy a sixteen-foot ladder, and rig up these long metal bars on a metal rod to create a makeshift pulley system for hanging the garlands. It was a miracle that it worked."

**On a Low-Budget Way to Make a High Floral Impact:** "Table garlands are gorgeous—they're fresh, green, fragrant, and way less expensive than having to do an arrangement on every table. You have so many options for the greenery—eucalyptus, bay leaves, light airy asparagus ferns, then add on pomegranates, kumquats, and persimmons, plus some garden roses. Berries are also really beautiful."

# FLOWER POWER

BOHEMIAN BLOSSOMS FOR THE *BREAKING BAD* BRIDE

## Savannah Miller on Faded Roses, Red Currants, and Her English Countryside Wedding

**On the Wildest of Wildflowers:** "There were tons of faded, tea-colored, dirty pink roses everywhere. Also, old fragrant English posies of herbs: rosemary, sage, and lavender. They smelled incredible. We had two huge grand archways made of roses—one that led to the clearing where we did the ceremony, and one that led back to the grounds for the party. Our florist did a lot of foraging in the hedgerows and incorporated all these native green countryside flowers, too. Everything was sensual and rich and sexy and raw. And my bouquet was a huge, tumbling arrangement of stephanotis and gardenias. Also, my husband surprised me by wearing a little floral crown of rowan berries, ivy, and rosemary."

**On Her Inspiration:** "The wedding was supposed to feel like a medieval feast. The party was in a giant teepee with fire pits in the middle—and dinner was served at huge long trestle tables covered in reindeer skins, grapes, apples, plums, red currants, blackberries, little horn cups, and loads of candles."

**On Her Fave Flower:** "I love roses. They are everything to me. I totally connect with them on a soulful level because they are fragile and strong all at once."

**On Regrets:** "If I could get married again, I would do two things differently. Number one: I wish we had measured my head before my wedding day, because the flower crown was too tight, and we had to loosen it at the last minute and it was slipping around. The second thing? I should have waited until my baby was a bit older. At the time, he was only six months and I had to spend most of the after party breastfeeding him in the teepee. I couldn't even drink champagne!"

## Meredith Melling on Flower Crowns, Chuppahs, and Crimson Anemones

**On Her Floral Vibe:** "When I was an editor at *Vogue,* I developed a taste for overgrown, haphazard, multicolored arrangements—natural, wild-looking bouquets. When my boyfriend, Zach, and I decided to get married, it was such a crazy time in my life. I was about to have a baby, my father was terminally ill, and I had recently started my own business. I didn't know if I was emotionally strong enough to do all these things at once. But when I decided to go through with it, I wanted crazy flowers to match. The palette was shades of crimson and purple with a few touches of fresh greenery thrown in: scarlet anemones, deep red ranunculus, violet clematis, white delphinium, eucalyptus leaves, and burgundy peonies."

**On Bouquets, Centerpieces, and Crowns:** "I wore a flower crown, had a long table decorated with floral centerpieces and a chuppah-like structure adorned with flowers for guests to take pictures in front of. I didn't have a bouquet, but at the end of the night, I collected all the flowers from the room, tied them with a ribbon, and threw it off my balcony. My eight-year-old daughter, Eloise, caught it."

**On the Ceremony:** "Instead of traditional vows, we asked our twenty closest friends and family to bring something nice to read about happiness, life, love, and chance. I recited the lyrics to a George Jones song and fell to pieces crying."

**On Her Favorite Flowers:** "Well, I was not very into flowers growing up. In high school, I wore a tacky gold and black dress to prom with nude gold-glitter panty hose. My boyfriend brought me a white rose corsage to match—that his florist had spray-painted gold! But at *Vogue*, I became very influenced by Anna Wintour. She loves flowers that are wild, romantic, and bursting. Lots of lilacs, roses, and ranunculus."

## Leilani Bishop on Pikake, Pyromania, and Birds of Paradise

**On Her Floral Vibe:** "We got married in Hawaii, where I'm from. It was a mellow beach bonfire vibe. There was a tent wrapped in vines and ginger, wapuhi, torches, palm fronds, birds of paradise. Also, there were lots of loose flowers everywhere, plumeria and little purple orchid flowers on the bar and the ground. I wore a loose gardenia behind my ear."

**On Spiritual Signs:** "My mom is an astrologer and I've been told I have a connection to the goddess of fire. On my wedding day, right before the ceremony, in the corner of the lawn, a huge fire started out of nowhere. My mom started screaming that it was a sign from the gods. I totally thought so too—I'm a very spiritual person. Then I was walking down the aisle and my dad whispered to me that he started the fire accidentally with his cigarette!"

**On Her Fave Flower:** "Pikake. It was named the 'flower of love' by a Hawaiian princess. It's musky and smells amazing when you dab it on the insides of your thighs and your neck."

## Abby Spector on Wine Bottles, Weird Penises, and Nixing a Professional Florist

**On Imperfection:** "We got married on a farm in western Massachusetts in the summer. We knew that we didn't want to have a professional florist. We knew that we wanted to do our own flowers to save money. From the start, I gave up the idea of having perfect, put-together flowers."

**On the Art of DIY:** "My mom is a gardener, and she spearheaded the whole thing. Instead of vases, we wanted simple bottles: I found a bunch on Craigslist and my mom gathered them up from all her friends. She even went through their recycling! She ended up with tons of wine, olive oil, and glass soda bottles, then soaked them overnight so the labels came off. She found a farm that sold buckets of

flowers for fifty dollars each, and bought four of them the day before the wedding. Then she went to the venue with all my aunts and cousins, and made an assembly line for the arranging. They used ferns to add greenery to my bouquet."

**On Her Fave Flowers:** "Honestly, I don't know anything about flowers. I'm not even a plant person. I don't even know the difference between marigolds and daffodils. All I know is that I didn't want to have these long flowers on the table. I still don't know even know what they're called, but they kind of reminded me of weird penises."

## CRIMSON AND CLOVER, OVER AND OVER

Feeling guilty about having to throw away all your perfect expensive flowers post-wedding? Enter Repeat Roses, a nationwide service that will work with your florist post-wedding to disassemble and repurpose your flowers so that that they may be gifted to a hospital, nursing home, or local composting facility. Check out repeatroses.com for more info.

# GRASS ROOTS

*Flowers Don't Have to Break the Bank*

You can absolutely do your own flowers if you are on a budget. I have seen brides spend half a million dollars decorating hotel ballrooms with rare blooms but often their flowers don't hold a candle to brides who went with a wholesale flower website source and vintage Coke bottles for vases. The average American woman spends around two thousand bucks on her wedding blooms. More money doesn't necessarily mean more beautiful—in fact, it can sometimes be downright tacky. A single peony in a tiny glass vase is so much more chic than a mammoth-sized arrangement. Beautiful floral décor has very little to do with having an abundance of flowers, and everything to do with nuance and a subtle eye for detail. One flower can be as powerful as twenty.

# SUSTAINABLE BLOSSOMS

*Know the Source of Your Flowers*

A few decades ago, flowers sold in the United States were mostly sourced nationally and from Holland. Back then times and tastes were simpler. The demand was for traditional blossoms—roses, tulips, hydrangeas—but in recent years, exotic flowers have become all the rage. Accommodating this change required a shift in where flowers were being sourced. Today, ninety percent of flowers sold in the United States are foreign imports from South America and the Netherlands. In fact, flowers from Ecuador and Colombia account for ninety percent of the roses, ninety-eight percent of the carnations, and ninety-five percent of the chrysanthemums sold in the United States. These countries are geographically near the equator and the climate allows for a pretty exceptional environment for commercial growing.

If having an ethical wedding is a priority for you, it's important to be mindful of where your flowers are being sourced from and the working conditions in their country of origin. Similar to conflict-free stones, flowers should be produced in safe and ethical environments, the labor standards should be just, and workers should be compensated appropriately. Unfortunately, this is not often the case. The International Labor Rights Forum has uncovered cases of exploitative labor practices within the floral industry.

The only way to be one hundred percent sure that your flowers were grown in bucolic conditions is to go out in the fields and pick them yourself. Otherwise, be mindful of where you're purchasing from. Don't feel shy asking your florist about the "roots" of your flowers.

# LEAN AND GREEN

Even if you are a cynical, unromantic type who would rather munch broken glass than roam wistfully through a rose garden, you should still have flowers at your wedding! Even if you are just going down to the courthouse in dungarees to get a certificate of marriage, grab a bodega bouquet of daisies on the way. Even if you are having a tiny ceremony in your living room with two people present, still scatter some rose petals on the parquet. Even if flowers make you sneeze and break out in hives, at least tuck a wee sprig of rosemary behind one ear! All things green represent good juju galore. Get it in spades while you can.

# CHAPTER 7

# JUST THE TWO OF US

## WHEN YOUR BEST FRIEND ENDS UP ON THE BACK BURNER

**I**MET A GUY I LIKE," I said to Lou. It was a few weeks after my first date with M, and we were drinking coffee on her stoop. Literally, at that moment, Wes Anderson walked by. We both watched him, a tiny little man in a tight pink suit, strut down the street, then disappear around First Avenue.

"So I met a guy I like," I said again. "He's cool. He's cute. He races cars."

"Nice," Lou said.

"No. I mean, really. Like he's a really good guy."

"Mmm," Lou said. She started chewing on a fingernail.

"Like I think I might marry him."

She laughed at that, and who could blame her, but it was the beginning of the end.

I'D MET Lou five years earlier, in the spring of 2004, at a party on the Lower East Side. I'd been hooking up with a guy named Dave, an assistant at ABC News. One night, Dave was working late and his best friend, John, was having people over, so I'd wandered over to his apartment. John was a skinny know-it-all who went to Vassar. He wore colored Nikes and had a goatee. Within an hour we were wasted on blue drinks singing "White Rabbit" into a karaoke machine. His apartment overlooked Delancey, and while I was singing, I noticed a pretty blonde smoking a cigarette on a balcony across the street. John called out his window, "Come over!" and minutes later she did. Even in crummy shorts and a tee she was a knockout—long gold hair, bee-stung lips, big brown eyes—part hipster rug rat, part hot-bod platinum sexpot.

"I'm over this heat," she announced to John. She yanked on her ponytail and flopped on the couch next to me.

"I'm over everything," I said into the karaoke mic.

She looked at me, I looked back, and I swear to God, a tiny little spark of crazy sexy insta-girl-crush chemistry crackled like a flame between us. Then she said, "Hey, I'm Lou," and I pretended not to know who she was, but *of course* I did. She was an actress. Her breakout movie—a campy rom-com—had come out the summer I graduated from college.

After that, we started bumping into each other around the neighborhood, at the coffee shop or the yoga studio. She would invite me to parties, or to go thrifting or get breakfast with her, but I'd decline every time. I found her beyond intimidating. Truthfully, my insecurity back then ran so deep, I couldn't believe she wanted to be my friend.

I was twenty-seven. I'd just quit my job at *Nylon* magazine and gone through a high-drama breakup. I was getting drunk or high or both all the time and blue-drink-fueled karaoke was standard weekend fodder. I remember that whole period of time the way you might remember a really subpar tapas meal, in lots of little bite-sized bits, all of them kind of gross and greasy. Lots of blow jobs, shopping sprees, barfing pinot noir.

Eventually I realized I had to stop partying, and yoga became my drug of choice. I used to show up at the studio in my pajamas and cry through half the class, but weirdly, Lou always seemed happy to see me.

One day in the changing room after class she asked what I'd been up to.

"Crazy week," I said. "My sister just had a baby. I was actually in the delivery room."

"Wow. How was *that*?"

"It was a bloodbath."

Her eyes went wide. "I *love* a bloodbath."

Finally, it was on. We couldn't stop talking. We talked about everything: penises, astral projection, Patti Smith. That weekend we had our first girl date: a road trip to her hometown where we ate dinner with her eccentric parents and slept in the same bed. As we drove home through the Holland Tunnel she dished some insider scoop on the whole Tom Cruise–Katie Holmes thing, gesticulating wildly with her chipped, cherry-painted nails.

A few months later she moved into an apartment across the street. Every morning we'd walk to the corner for coffee, drink it on the stoop in pajamas. At night we'd hit premieres and parties. Saturday afternoons were for roaming the Lower East Side arm in arm, wearing matching purple heart sunglasses, reciting lines from *Fight Club*.

I was in love.

One day we bought a taxidermied cow's head at a thrift store. When we got home, we realized that it smelled like rancid manure. Lou decided we should boil it to kill the stench. She said, "Here's the plan," and emerged from under her sink wearing big rubber gloves. She submerged the skull into a pot, then stood over the stove prodding it with a wooden stick. I couldn't stop laughing.

Once she texted me in the middle of the night to help remove a mouse from her toaster.

Once she texted me in the middle of the day to come see a YouTube clip of Susan Boyle singing "I Dreamed a Dream" and we sat there watching it and blinking back tears.

Once at a party she threw at her apartment, she started telling me how great her gynecologist was. "Can you send me her info?" I asked. Lou's response was "She's right over there!" and pointed to a chic brunette drinking a martini.

Lou taught me to cry on command. She taught me that hotel room pornography could be written off as a work expense. That you could act like the most important person in the room by ignoring everyone.

I taught her about my favorite alterna-girl pop culture icons, like Mary Gaitskill and Fiona Apple, and the differences between Jungian and Freudian analysis, and how consuming nine fish oil vitamins daily was scientifically proven to boost serotonin levels.

Our differences were almost comical. She was the intrepid Jersey Girl who knew Morse code and once hiked the Himalayas on a whim. I was the depressive Pisces and unemployed writer, holed up inside my head. She had an agent and a lawyer and a publicist and a manager and a business manager. I had two cats (one was on Prozac), and my parents were paying half my rent.

When Lou wasn't out of town filming, her social life was an endless string of movie premieres, parties, after-parties, and fashion shows, and I got to be her wingwoman. I'd get ready and walk over to her apartment, then lie on the couch while a makeup artist agonized over her eyeliner. After events, I'd go home and google her name to see if I ended up in any of the party photos.

A few years passed and Lou made more movies. She traveled to Paris, Alaska, Mexico City. And I . . . well, I kept doing my thing, which was not much. I went to grad school, took weird freelance writing jobs, and babysat for my professor. She had a constant rotating lazy Susan of boyfriends, most of them famous, rich, and hot—a far cry from the hobos I was hooking up with. There was the shaggy pop star with a private jet, the ex–sitcom celeb with an infinity pool. She was focused on work though. She was someone who claimed to never want to get married and you actually believed her. *"Who cares?"* she said once when I brought it up. "Look at Diane Keaton!"

LOU WAS the first friend I called after getting engaged. She was on set; I was on my lunch break. "M proposed last night!" I screamed into the phone, standing on the corner of Fifty-Seventh and Seventh. A second later I regretted it.

"I'm so happy for you!" she said, but it was strained and theatrical. She'd met M only once before leaving for Toronto to film a TV pilot. During that time I'd given up my apartment and moved to Brooklyn with M.

Awkward small talk ensued, then I fudged an excuse as to why I had to hang up.

When Lou came back to town, she did everything right. We picked out registry items and brainstormed venues together. I asked her to help me find a makeup artist and she gave me the best, most Lou-worthy advice ever: *dewy cheeks and lipstain,* call it a day. But there was a flat, anxious vibe to it all. The deliciously kinetic energy we'd once had together had suddenly dried up.

Then two months before the wedding she broke her leg doing a stunt on set. It was a bad break. She was airlifted from Toronto to New York, where I met her at the hospital. Weeks passed and while I was running around the city in full wedding planning mode, Lou was holed up in her living room in a wheelchair, surrounded by dusty stacks of scripts and tended to by a caretaker in uniform.

I came over one day with a container of soup and a favor to ask. Could I do my wedding dress fittings in her apartment, since the seamstress was in Manhattan and I didn't want to keep dragging the dress back to Brooklyn? She was clearly annoyed. For a while we sat in silence watching shadows from the trees outside snake across the ceiling.

"Sorry, Lou," I said.

"It's fine," she said.

"You're my best friend," I said.

She didn't respond to that.


THE MORNING of the wedding Lou showed up at my hotel suite with coffee and helped me steam the dress. Even as an invalid she looked fresh off the pages of *French Vogue:* her bun was slicked, her black dress was tiny, and her lips were the perfect shade of bright red. With her leg encased in plaster from ankle to thigh, she looked like a bizarre Helmut Newton–Barbie hybrid. In a cruel twist of scheduling fate, the wedding actually fell on her birthday, and when I handed her a pathetic gift (an artisanal beer bottle opener made with antlers) on the limo ride to the venue with my mom and Becca, she said "Aww" but didn't make eye contact. During the ceremony, she teetered up to the mic on her crutches, and recited a Raymond Carver poem about butterflies. But during the party, I caught her staring into space after the speeches, looking dreamy and dark and ready to leave. Later that night, as I was packing for the honeymoon, she texted, *You did so great today. Elegant, warm, beautiful, and true* but again it felt forced. Then months passed, and despite a few halfhearted attempts to connect over email, we never talked again.

WHAT HAPPENED? Who knows. Maybe our relationship was grossly imbalanced from the start. Maybe I loved Lou more than she loved me. Maybe we were always doomed since she was famous and I wasn't. Maybe it was all of those things and none of those things. I think, most likely, it had to do with the fact that our friendship rested on me always being her plus one. I didn't have much of a life when Lou and I were hanging out. Then, suddenly I did—and the whole friendship fell apart.

Best girlfriend heartbreak can be so much harder than any other kind. The connection is purely heart to heart, and in some ways you're more vulnerable with your girlfriends than with anybody. When things go south, there's no protocol. There's no breakup talk or revenge sex or closure. You can't just go to the bar and pound shots and scream, "He's a dick." Sometimes there's just a shift, and you don't really know why.

I do know that during my first year of marriage I needed a best friend more than ever. I was mourning the freedom of my old life—those late sexy nights when Lou and I were walking to a cool party, arm in arm, feeling that a new adventure was about to unfold around every corner. The novelty of being married was magical, but I weirdly missed all those aimless hours of thrifting and laughing hysterically and standing around at parties, people watching and wasting time. Most of all, I missed Lou. She was one of my great loves.

ONE NIGHT a couple years later, I was in bed thumbing through a gossip site on my phone and there was Lou. She'd gone and gotten married after all. Sparkly dress, flowy veil, armful of dahlias. It all came back then, my late twenties, John and Dave, *Fight Club* quotes, the East Village, all of it. The years I'd spent sinking into the muck of my own solipsism and how Lou waltzed in, yanked me out, then turned and walked away.

Feeling emotional, and pissed off not to have been invited, I got out of bed and snuggled up next to M on the couch. He was watching *Deadliest Catch* and eating cheddar bunnies.

"Lou got married, babe," I said.

"Cool," he said, his eyes glued to the screen.

"My feelings are so hurt! We weren't even invited!"

"Who cares," he said, reaching for another handful of bunnies. "You haven't talked to her in years."

I debated launching into a monologue about how devastated I was—but then decided against it. *Deadliest* is literally M's church, plus he probably wouldn't have understood anyway. Your husband is *not* your best friend, despite what people might say.

## GIRLS, GIRLS, GIRLS

If you haven't already guessed, I'm a big-time believer in the power of sisterhood. My best female friendships have guided me through many a dark night of the soul. I love my bitches. They are my everything.

Friendship. It's a strange, sacred thing. A series of fits and starts: There's no ritual to cement it, no formula for maintaining it. It's a wild by-product of chemistry, history, and circumstance. I've fought and fallen out with almost all of my girlfriends—like, literally stopped talking for years—only to reconnect later on in completely unexpected circumstances. Often we ended up closer than ever.

Meeting your life partner and getting married will, without fail, affect your friendships. Platonic intimacy and romantic intimacy can be hard to reconcile, but I promise you, it can be done. With a lot of sensitivity, mindfulness, and extra-special girl-bonding sessions, your friendship can definitely survive the transition.

# RULES FOR FRIENDSHIP SURVIVAL

## 1. NOT ALL LOVE IS CREATED EQUAL

Do not demote your best friend when you get married. That whole "husband-as-best-friend" thing is weird propaganda that only exists in Paul Rudd movies. Your husband is not your best friend! Repeat after me! Your husband is your husband! Your best friend is your best friend. They should fulfill two totally different roles in your life. Your husband is your lover, your life partner, your co-homeowner/renter, and (maybe) your co-parenter. Your best friend is the person who knows your every weirdest, darkest secret, who is always there to bitch to over a glass of wine, who immediately understands how you're feeling, and who knew you before you were married. You need her now more than ever. Plus, when you keep your best friendships strong, there's less pressure on your husband to fulfill all your emotional needs.

## 2. MAKE ROOM FOR CHANGE

So things will be different between you and your BF. You're now sharing your space and your life with someone else full-time. Some (or all) of your crazy codependent text messages, phone calls, and marathon hangout sessions will probably become things of the past. That's normal. If, all of a sudden, you experience a ton of tension, trust that it's part of the process. Even though your impulse might be to say, "Fuck this, I can't deal," remember that you can. Breathe through the discomfort. Time will tell what happens next. You will most likely hit your BF stride again soon.

### 3.   TALK IT OUT . . .

Create a safe space to discuss your fears. Invite your BF out for a drink and open up the floor to shoot the shit about the crazy changes happening in your life. Maybe your friend is really secure and is like, *Great! Peace out. Love that you met your soulmate. Let me know when you want to hang next.* But, most likely, she will be feeling some mixed emotions—happy for you, but sad that your friendship is changing. Don't judge her for that. Say something like: *Yes, I met this guy and I'm getting married, but I still love you. You're my best friend, and I need you. Our friendship is going to go through an insane transition, but we're going to weather it together.* Then get wasted and google penis pics of Orlando Bloom.

### 4.   . . . BUT DON'T DISH DIRT

You can absolutely use your best friend as a sounding board to talk about the deep, dark stuff in your marriage—but check yourself before you do it. If something really stressful is going on or you haven't seen your friend in a while, your impulse might be to unload and dive right into some juicy personal gossip. But ask yourself if you're being confessional just for the sake of being confessional . . . and if this is really information that needs to be shared. You might not want to talk about the scary health issues your mother-in-law is having, or money troubles your husband is experiencing. Ask yourself: *How would I feel if the tables were turned and my husband was sharing these things about me?* Absolutely confide in your friend if these things are directly affecting you and you need advice. But blabbing on just out of boredom? Not cool. Have boundaries, baby.

### 5.   BE MINDFUL

You might feel like your world has just turned upside down, but that doesn't give you license to talk only about yourself! In fact, you should try doing the opposite: Invite your friend to dinner, apologize in advance for being so self-centered lately, and spend the night asking questions about her life and actually listening to what she has to say (instead of waiting until it's your turn to talk about yourself). Once, when I was having a crisis at work and had been talking about myself nonstop for months, I took my friend Rachel to brunch, set my phone timer for thirty minutes, told her to fill me in on everything going on in her life, and put a piece of masking tape over my mouth. I also recommend scheduling bimonthly girl dates. P.S.: You are absolutely forbidden from ever even suggesting that you bring your husband out on a girl date!

## 6. GIVE UP THE FIGHT

If your BF and your husband just don't like each other, it's not up to you to force them into a friendship. It's a terrible situation for sure, but it's made a hundred times worse when you make them hang out with you at the same time. Best thing to do is to acknowledge it: "I know that you don't like _____, but he's my guy and this is hard for me to navigate. Please just try to be pleasant when you see him and remember how important he is to me." You may need to make a similar appeal to your husband. Then take a deep breath and let it go.

## 7. FLY SOLO

It's hard to have an honest, uncensored convo in your apartment when your husband is home—so why not kick him out of the house every now and then? Tell him to plan a guys' night, or coordinate when he's out of town for a business trip, so that you can have some alone time in your own space with your girlfriends. Toss some pillows on the floor, pop open some wine, order Chinese takeout, and make like it's old times.

# CLINICAL PSYCHOLOGIST LEIGH KEISER ON HOW TO FALL IN LOVE WITHOUT BREAKING YOUR BEST FRIEND'S HEART

**On How Marriage Changes Best Friendship:** "Best friends rely on each other for everything. They hold each other's hopes and dreams. They know the ins and outs of each other's desires. When one friend is suddenly madly in love with another person, it drastically changes the dynamic. It can get very complicated. My best friend in my twenties knew what I wanted for my life. Everything from what I wanted to wear, to how stressed I got when my mom called. All the mundane stuff, all the profound stuff. The love between women is so strong."

**On Identity in Your Twenties:** "In your twenties your identity is shifting and you are becoming an individual. Up to this point, your family has been your main source of identity — even if the relationship has been complex and difficult. Suddenly, you're living on your own or with roommates. You evolve into yourself, and part of that process is separating from your early family identity. It's scary to navigate this alone — and often your female friendships become really charged as you bond over the drama and pain of self-discovery. You share your hopes, dreams, and fears with your close friends. You're your most vulnerable with them. So it's really scary when one person falls in love and gets married. It can feel like being abandoned."

**On Incorporating Your Best Friend into the Wedding Process:** "Don't leave her out of the planning. If she loves fashion, have her try on dresses with you. If she has great taste, run décor ideas by her. And lean on her during the wedding day . . . that's what bridesmaids and maids of honor are for! I actually had one of my best friends officiate the wedding, which was really special. And prior to the ceremony, make sure to squeeze her hand and have a moment together."

**On Letting Go:** "Transitions are hard. It's okay if there's some sadness — your friendship is changing and you don't know what the future holds. Sometimes friendships don't last. It doesn't mean that they weren't true friendships. It means that they served a specific purpose for a specific time in your life."

# MAMA — ME — AGH!!!!!

*Belligerent one-word answers and eye rolls need not apply.*
*Even if she's driving you batshit, don't forget to treat your mom*
*with lots of kindness and compassion.*

I know it's a trying relationship. I know she has no boundaries and projects her past failures on your future successes and forgot to pick you up on the playground that one time in third grade when there also happened to be a hailstorm. I'm sure you've spent years on the therapist's couch analyzing every inch of your relationship, but let's not use your wedding planning experience as another trigger for past traumas. It wasn't that long ago that your mother was your anchor. Your main source of emotional stability. But that's all in the past now, and it's painful and unspoken and both you and she know it. I have a vivid memory of asking my mom to marry me when I was five, and meaning it with my whole heart. Seems so silly now; at the time it was everything.

Ask your mom to go dress shopping with you . . . at least once. Send her links to dresses that *she* might wear while she's walking down the aisle. Ask her questions about her own wedding in earnest. Email her the sample menu with the subject line: "Would love to hear your thoughts!" Let her know she is needed. Honestly, she probably doesn't care that much about your napkin color or cut of beef, but she does want to be part of the conversation. And don't underestimate the power of saying: "I love you so much, Mom. Thank you for everything."

P.S.: If your mom's a total bitch, disregard this paragraph.

# FRIENDS WITH BENEFITS

## MARRIAGE MADE THESE BEST FRIENDS STRONGER.

**Carrie Goldberg:** "I met Sarah in college in student government and we became best friends right away. After college I stayed in New York while she moved to Pittsburgh, but we made a pact to never be apart for more than eight weeks, and we've kept it up, even since she's gotten married. Without fail, every two months, we trade off visiting each other. In New York, we spend the weekend doing a marathon gallery and museum crawl, and in Pittsburgh we go to every vintage and antiques store under the sun. Her husband totally supports it—I stay at their house when I'm there."

**Rachel Fleit:** "I met Sonia after she started dating my friend Sandy. The three of us became really close—and when they got married, they folded me right into their family. Every summer they rent a house in Vermont and I go and stay with them for a week. We have epic barbecues and swim for hours in the lake. The last time I visited them in LA they took me with them on their Saturday date night—to the Hollywood Museum, then to dinner, and then to a chick flick. It was so emotional that Sonia and I held hands and cried the whole time. Sandy left halfway through."

**Tali Magal:** "Becky's husband, Gavin, and I went to college together, then we lost touch when I moved to New York. Ten years later I heard that Gavin had moved to town and I went to see him perform with his band. He was adamant that I meet his fiancée. He kept telling me I would love her—and I rolled my eyes, thinking *yeah right,* but the next time we got together, Becky and I blew right past hitting it off. We danced all night. Everyone faded out. The whole time we were in hysterics. Then Gavin became fast friends with my fiancé, Craig, and for years we all tore up the town, hung out, and traveled together. Eventually Craig and I moved to Dumbo, and Becky and Gavin stayed in the city, but a few years later they bought an apartment in our building. It sounds so hokey but it's heaven. They're on the second floor and we're on the seventh. In the depths of the winter freeze, when it's three degrees out, I toss on my bedroom slippers and go downstairs for a hang. We have each other's keys. If we don't know what to do for dinner we call down and ask: 'What are we ordering?' It's constant built-in plans with great friends any night of the week."

# THE LIGHT AT THE
# (FRI)END OF THE TUNNEL

If you've lost touch with your best friend somewhere along the wedding planning process, don't lose faith. Best friends are, in a way, best friends forever . . . whether or not you want them to be. And when it comes to relationships, there is never a *real* end to any story. Who knows, maybe Lou and I will end up on the dining room deck of the same seaside nursing home when we're ninety-seven, sitting side by side in driftwood chairs and sharing a bowl of Jell-O cubes. Remembering the crazy days way back when, squinting against the sun.

# CHAPTER 8

# I DO

## CREATING A KICKASS WEDDING CEREMONY

COBBLING TOGETHER OUR CEREMONY was my favorite part of the wedding planning process—probably because I'm a self-involved dork who embraces all opportunities to think about herself. I know that this is not everyone's cup of tea and completely understand the appeal of reciting traditional vows. Personally, I was super into the process of curating my favorite songs, poems, and people and creating a little performance that communicated the power of everlasting love.

M could not have cared less. He would have been happy to go by the book and have a typical Irish-Catholic wedding in a church. Unluckily for him, every Sunday for months I dragged him with me to meet my rabbi, Amichai, at a restaurant in the East Village to talk religion and infidelity and finances and childrearing. Poor guy. We also had to sit down with his parents, my parents, and Amichai to talk about creating an inclusive wedding ceremony that honored both our backgrounds. This was the first time our parents met, and we covered a lot of ground: Jesus, Judaism, holy water, the works. In the end, we decided to build a ceremony that was more literary than religious, although there were some really important elements of a Jewish wedding that I wanted to incorporate—the seven

blessings, the signing of the ketubah, the chuppah (M built it out of birch branches), and the breaking of the glass. My father-in-law read a Gaelic prayer about love. A couple of our friends read poems. We wrote our own vows. M sang my favorite Nick Cave song, "Rock of Gibraltar," and he was really nervous, which made it all the more sweet.

What I learned in the process is that there is nothing cool about a wedding ceremony—and that is a good thing. My wedding ceremony made me feel vulnerable and happy and excited: walking down the aisle on my dad's arm while he cried, holding M's hands and staring into his eyes, struggling to keep it together under the chuppah when Becca read my nana's *Tips for a Happy Marriage* (she'd died six weeks earlier). The whole experience lacked irony and sarcasm and cynicism and it was *awesome.* Who knew?

A wedding ceremony is a total performance—like wild Kabuki theater. You're giving your guests a tremendous gift—allowing them to step out of the messy jumble of their lives, suspend disbelief, forget about their taxes and their pinworm prescriptions and the fact that their feet hurt. You're restoring their faith in romance, in the miracle of two people finding each other, and falling in love. So own that. Today you stand for everyone else's new beginning. It's a beautiful thing.

# FIVE WAYS TO ENSURE YOU DON'T CHECK OUT WHILE SAYING YOUR VOWS

## 1. STAY PRESENT

There was a moment during my ceremony when I glanced into the audience and saw my friend Adina splayed out in her chair, staring at the ceiling, and sighing deeply. I totally lost my concentration and started obsessing: "Adina is bored! I'm so boring. What a terrible time everyone must be having . . ." When I mentioned it to her a few weeks later she responded: "No way! I was so overcome with emotion at how beautiful everything was that I was just trying to keep it together!" Typical of me to go down the rabbit hole of stinking thinking at such a pivotal moment. Take it as a cautionary tale. If you start to worry what people are thinking, catch yourself and come back to the moment. Most likely your guests are thinking about love as it relates to their own lives—and NOT about how your arms look fat in your dress.

## 2. EMBRACE CHAOS

There is no such thing as the Fourth Wall when it comes to a wedding ceremony. It's an interactive experience. If someone's phone rings, don't be afraid to acknowledge it lightheartedly. If your groom starts sobbing, ask your guests for a hanky. All the unexpected variables can make for some incredibly poignant, personal moments. At one point during our ceremony, my girlfriend Britney's two-year-old daughter, Rita, wandered up to the chuppah and started crying, so I picked her up and held her until she quieted down.

### 3.   OWN YOUR EMOTIONS

There is no textbook way to get through your vows. Whether you're sensitive and teary, focused and stoic, blissful and calm, or vibrating with nervous energy, give yourself permission to feel it, embrace it, and own it. Take a deep breath, look into your partner's eyes, and speak clearly. Contrary to popular belief (and although it might feel counterintuitive), taking your time and talking at your own pace is actually a pretty effective way to quell nerves.

### 4.   MAKE EYE CONTACT . . . WITH EVERYONE

Of course you'll be looking longingly into your partner's eyes, but don't forget to look out at your guests, too. It's really special to lock gazes with the important people in your life—even if it's just for half a second.

### 5.   SOUND OFF

I've sat through ceremonies where I couldn't hear a thing, and it's pretty boring to stare at two people's lips moving. Best to have a wireless mic handy, even if you think you are great at speaking clearly and projecting. Always better to be safe than silent.

# A SHAMAN, A REVEREND, AND A RABBI

### THESE THREE OFFICIANTS ALL SPEAK
### THE LANGUAGE OF LOVE.

## Universal Life Church Officiant Amanda Capobianco
## on Exorcisms, Blessings, and Bubbles

**On Getting Ordained:** "I got ordained online at the Universal Life Church. Once you're ordained, you can also do exorcisms!"

**On Creating Rituals:** "When I work with a couple, I set up an initial consultation and ask them about their vision for the ceremony. I get to know them—their story, how they met, what their lives are like, what they do for a living. I explain that the ceremony is essentially a series of rituals meant to bring your guests and family together. Family and friends speaking on your behalf, a series of blessings. Anything can be a blessing. A champagne toast is a blessing wrapped in bubbles. I also ask the couple what they might want to incorporate from their family background and what they want to stay away from."

**On the Elements:** "Most of my couples want to honor the spirits beyond themselves. We do this by acknowledging the four essential elements, which represent the four sacred gateways of the earth. Often this is done at the beginning of any sacred rite to call in protection and blessings."

**On God:** "I once did a honey-drinking ritual in late summer. The bride was Catholic and the groom had no religion. He didn't feel comfortable with the word 'god,' so we used the word 'spirit' instead. At the end, they each drank the wine as the sacrament of Christ, and then two little shot glasses of honey, which represented the sweetness of the start of their life together."

**On Vows:** "I once officiated a wedding on the beach in Indonesia, and was standing so close to the couple that I could literally feel their nerves. They recited these gorgeous vows—'I offer you peace, I offer you love, I offer you friendship. I see your beauty, I hear your needs, I feel your feelings. All wisdom flows from the highest source. I honor that source in you.' There was so much love between these two people—I had the best seat in the house."

## Interfaith Minister Reverend Annie Lawrence on Seminary School, Surprise Vows, and Smashing Pumpkins

**On Becoming a Minister:** "When I first moved to New York, I discovered an interfaith seminary called The New Seminary where we looked at gods and goddesses of the world and we began to write rituals for life's big moments—birth, marriage, death—and I thought, *THIS is how I can contribute to the world.* So I enrolled in seminary school. The first wedding I did was for the niece of a friend who was getting married at Bear Mountain. Instead of a reading from Shakespeare or scripture, she wanted to recite lyrics from the Smashing Pumpkins. I thought it was an apt choice that reflected her personality—all music is poetry, anyway."

**On Creating the Perfect Ceremony:** "When I meet with a couple, I first ask them how they want to spend their time with me. Some people are very shy and private, and others want to tell me their whole love story. I ask them how and where they met, their first impressions of one another, what they love about each other, how they're alike and how they're different, and what their hopes and plans for the future are. I want to know what they want to tell their partner on their wedding day, and then I write a story about them. I ask couples to describe how they see their weddings in their minds' eye. Some will say, 'Elegant, traditional, classic.' Others will say, 'Silly, fun, relaxed.' "

**On Choosing Songs and Readings:** "It varies. Some couples choose readings from the movie *Love Actually,* some people quote Carrie Bradshaw. I've cued songs by the Beatles and Justin Timberlake. I've seen brides walk down the aisle to the Smiths and to a violin. One of my personal favorites was a reading from *Captain Corelli's Mandolin.*"

**On Vows:** "I have a three-paragraph formula for writing your own vows. The first one is 'You,' which is praise for your partner: 'You're so beautiful, you're so fabulous. You excite me. You make my life better.' The second paragraph is 'Me': 'I feel so blessed. I feel so grateful. I feel like I'm a better person because of you.' The third paragraph is 'Us': 'Together, we're going to travel the world and have exciting adventures. We're going to have quiet time and get to know each other better and get older and wiser. We're going to have a wonderful future.' Some couples write their vows together side by side, so that they're really balanced and parallel. To other couples, I say, 'If you want to keep your vows private and surprise each other on your wedding day, email me privately. I will read your vows side by side and give you feedback.' For example, if his are really funny, I'll say to the bride, 'You need to say something funny about him.' If hers are really romantic, I'll say to him, 'Hey, you're leaning a little on the funny side. We all appreciate your sense of humor, but you have to say something romantic about how wonderful she is.' It should not be expected that you memorize your vows. That's way too much pressure on your wedding day."

**On Getting Married Again:** "In my parents' generation, people renewed their vows at fifty years. These days, I get calls from people I married two or three years ago who ask me if I can marry them again. They say, 'We've had a tough year and life is stressful.' And I think that's amazing. You don't just say these words to each other once. You should say them over and over again in as many ways as you need to. If you're in Vegas, go get your vows renewed by Elvis, or if you're in Hawaii go get married again on the beach. Relive that once-in-a-lifetime moment as much as you can."

# Psychoanalyst Ellen Lewis on Relationships, Rites of Passage, and Rings

**On Ritual and Tradition:** "All couples want their wedding to be unique. They all want it to feel personal, so they think they have to create a ceremony from scratch. But rituals exist for a reason. A ritual is like a vessel that you pour yourself into. And it is entirely possible to create a unique and personalized ceremony by incorporating old rituals. In the Jewish wedding, you are telescoping two ancient ceremonies, the engagement and the marriage, into one. There is real value in relying on ritual. It's not there to limit you—it's there to free you, to create joy."

**On the Ceremony:** "No Jewish ceremony should last longer than twenty minutes. A traditional ceremony begins with comments and then a ketubah signing. A ketubah is basically a Jewish wedding contract, an agreement that the couple is making within the context of the Jewish tradition, promising themselves to each other. The signing of the ketubah can be public or private. Then there's a welcome, a blessing over the sacredness of the marriage, two wine blessings, and the exchange of the rings. In traditional Judaism, the man used to give the ring to the woman—it was a property transaction in which the man was acquiring the woman. Today, most people like to make that process more egalitarian, and so the couple will give each other rings symbolizing their commitment to one another. Then there are the seven benedictions. This is where you can incorporate your friends and family. I like to do these prayers in both Hebrew and in English. Some couples worry that if there is too much Hebrew their guests will feel alienated. To that I respond: 'Treat your guests like they are smart, not stupid!' Then there is the breaking of the glass. The most common explanation for this ritual is that we live in a shattered world, but that the couple is a symbol of wholeness. When conflict or tragedy arises in their lives down the road, the idea is that they can think back to this moment when everything was in harmony."

**On Premarital Counseling:** "Everyone has issues when planning a wedding. There is a fundamental issue of separation that happens when two people are moving toward each other, and away from their family of origin. Relationships change and a lot of this gets played out in the planning of the wedding. It's very important to be cognizant of the shifts that are occurring here. I like to meet with couples three to four times before the wedding and I start by asking them what they're worried about. If it's the flowers, we talk about the flowers. If it's who is going to walk them down the aisle, we talk about that. Inevitably, no matter where you start, you will end up talking about the things that are the most important. I don't believe in imposing topics like money or sex. And it's important to get comfortable with the idea of talking to a third party when things get difficult. It plants the seeds for down the road when hard issues come up."

## QUESTIONS TO ASK WHEN CHOOSING AN OFFICIANT

"Does their personality and philosophy match ours?"

"Are they warm and inviting?"

"Are they going to take time to get to know you and your love story?"

"Are they going to be reading directly from a book or will they be addressing you?"

"Are they on time and prepared?"

"Will they be there to help you do a walk-through?"

"Can they recommend musicians, photographers, makeup artists so that your wedding team is all on the same page?"

## RICE IS NICE

There's something super sweet about the old school post-wedding rice toss tradition. Like most bizarre marriage rituals, no one quite knows how it originated (it's rumored that the pagans thought that the grain could transfer fertility to the newlywed couple), but these days it's as prevalent as ever. (By the way, that whole thing about how tossed rice kills birds? Total urban legend.) It's a win-win for everyone: makes for great photos, creates a festive vibe, plus all your agro bridesmaids get to work out their rage. For a bit more color, add in dried rose petals and lavender. It'll photograph well and smell heavenly. Just make sure to grab Grandma's arm on the way out of the church. Dry rice can get a little slippery underfoot.

# STAND ON CEREMONY

## WHEN IT COMES TO THE FABRIC OF LOVE, THESE FIVE COUPLES ARE ALL CUT FROM THE SAME CLOTH.

### The City Hall Ceremony

"The morning of our wedding it started pissing rain," says photographer Frances Tulk-Hart, who married her husband, Jason Rossi, in a summer wedding at City Hall in New York City. "I was seven months pregnant and nervous as hell. Jason went to the dry cleaners to get some buttons sewn back on his shirt, and I got dressed in my tight Alexander Wang dress. It was the first time in my life I had boobs and a butt, and I was determined to show them off. On the way to City Hall, we picked up Starbucks. The rain was coming down like crazy and we were huddled under a tiny pink umbrella. My hair looked like an orange pom-pom from the humidity. Once we got to City Hall, we had to wait in a long line. It was like being at the butcher. I giggled the whole way through the five-minute ceremony. Then we hopped in the car again and started driving upstate. My whole family followed us, and we stopped off Route 87 and grabbed Burger King."

# The Mountaintop Ceremony

"I married Scott on a hillside in Sunshine Canyon, in the mountains outside of Boulder," says outdoor apparel designer Jenny Uehisa, who married her husband, a long-distance runner, in Colorado. "We planned it as a big summer party for our friends and two weeks before the wedding there was a huge fire in the Boulder foothills. But thankfully the fires were put out, rainstorms came and cleared the air. That morning we went for a

morning trail run up Flagstaff Mountain with a big group of friends. Nothing like running in 100-degree heat at a high altitude to sweat out a hangover! My dad walked me down an aisle made of fallen branches and pinecones. After we exchanged vows, our friend, Brett, played an acoustic version of his song, 'She's Mine,' and my friend Caroline played my favorite song from the movie *Amélie*, 'Comptine d'un autre été: L'après-midi,' on her upright piano."

## The Blended Ceremony (Hin-Jew)

"First we had a Mehndi, a small gathering where the family applied intricate henna designs to my hands and feet," says Dr. Deepika Chopra, who married her Jewish husband, Alex, in Palo Alto in the summer. "Then we had a chura, where a set of red and white bangles were given to me to wear on the wedding day. It was followed by the tying of kaleeras (gold ornaments) to my wrists. Then my relatives smeared me in traditional turmeric paste. My husband-to-be rode into the venue on an adorned white horse with a mobile DJ, three Indian drummers, and all his friends and family. Then the 'Milni' took place, which literally means 'to meet.' Alex and my family exchanged garlands, hugged and accepted each other as a part of their own. Then the guests made their way to the ceremony. On each seat was a smooth stone and everyone was asked to write a quick blessing for us. My younger female cousins showered Alex and his family with flower petals, while five Hindu pundits chanted my favorite mantra, the *Gayatri Mantra*. My close cousins escorted me down the aisle, holding the sides of my mother's dupatta like a canopy. They led me to my maternal grandfather, who brought me over to my father and my little sister. I took my shoes off so that I could proceed to enter the sacred mandap. Next, our dear family friend recited some beautiful Rumi poems and Hebrew blessings to honor Alex's father."

# The Buddhist Ceremony

"Nick and I got engaged in July and set our wedding date for November 13, just four months later," says Emily Ziff Griffin, who married her husband in his parents' house in the hills of Los Angeles. "We were determined to focus primarily on what marriage meant to us, so we asked his uncle Kevin, who is a Buddhist meditation teacher, to lead our ceremony. We had sixty-five guests on a small patch of grass in Nick's parents' backyard. Our three flower girls who wore whatever they wanted and each carried a single calla lily. I carried three flowers tied with the same twine that Nick used to make me a ring when he spontaneously proposed. We walked down the aisle without music. Kevin instructed everyone that photos would not be allowed during the ceremony because we wanted everyone's full presence. He then led us all in a brief meditation that focused on the concept of 'mudita,' which is joy at the joy of others. We asked Kevin to read aloud the names of the important people who had passed away, including my father. We had two readings, both poems about the transcendent power of nature. One was 'Inventing a Horse' read and written by my friend Meghan O'Rourke and the other was 'We Two— How Long We Were Fool'd' by Walt Whitman."

# The Jew-ISH Ceremony

"I'm an East Coast Jew who still misses summer camp and goes home to my parents' house every Passover and Rosh Hashanah," says Danya, founder of ARQ (a lifestyle brand inspired by Jewish culture), who married Andrew in the Green Building in Brooklyn. "Andrew is a Christmas-loving, bacon-eating West Coast guy who's spiritual. We agreed on a Jewish ceremony, but we didn't want it to feel dry or impersonal. We lucked out big-time with our rabbi, Jim Ponet. Right before the ceremony, we signed our ketubah, the Jewish marriage contract. Rather than use the traditional language, which refers to the bride's dowry and the marriage as an acquisition of the bride by the groom from the bride's father, we worked with our rabbi to write up original text in English and Hebrew. Andrew walked down the aisle to 'La Vie en Rose' played by Louis Armstrong since his father, who passed away, loved Louis. I walked down the aisle to 'Love Is Here to Stay' written by Gershwin. We stood under a chuppah covered in greenery and my grandfather's prayer shawl. Its four open walls represented our future home. Traditionally, the bride circles the groom seven times to show that he is the focal point of her life, but, being a lot more egalitarian in our relationship, we split the circling in half and then circled each other at the same time for the final round. In our wedding program, we encouraged everyone, after the glass was smashed, to shout 'Mazel Tov!' which literally translates to 'Your fortune has been good.' Immediately afterward, we followed the Jewish tradition of yichud and spent a few minutes alone before entering the reception."

## SUPER HERO

*How Do You Bribe Your Unruly Nephew to Walk Those Rings Down the Aisle? Let Him Wear His Underoos!*

"Our nephew Lucas is just the sweetest, most kindhearted kid," says Of a Kind founder Claire Mazur, who got married in her parents' backyard in Delaware. "When we asked him if he would be the ring bearer we told him he could wear whatever he wanted. At that stage he was wearing superhero costumes daily, and Spider-Man was the going favorite. He was the first one to walk out in the processional in his costume, and of course everyone lit up with laughter."

# FOR CRYING OUT LOUD

THESE SIX COUPLES SAID THEIR "I DO'S"
AMIDST A BEAUTIFUL MESS.

"At our Memphis wedding, Dan (Adam's brother) pronounced us 'Adam and Adina' because I refused to let him say 'man and wife.' Adam's very traditional grandfather shouted, 'They're not married 'til you pronounce them man and wife!' So I lost that battle."

—ADINA GRIGORE

"Since my father died in 2005 I had my younger brother walk me down the aisle. Our chuppah was handmade by my friend Carrie, who also did the flowers. We hired the Raya Brass Band, a self-described 'exuberant Balkan from Brooklyn,' to play at our wedding reception. It's all a blur, but I think he played drums and accordion."

—MARY PATTERSON

"My father passed away ten weeks before the wedding. Around the same time, after a long journey through various fertility treatments, we ended up getting married when I was nine weeks pregnant. When my doctor found out, he asked if I'd ever heard the term 'transmigration of souls.' Before I could reply I had tears streaming down my face as I knew he was referring to my father. My twin sister was my maid of honor and my brother gave me away as we walked down the grass to Sigur Rós's 'Hoppípolla.'"

—NICOLA GLASS

"Our ceremony was at Grace Church in New York. I had nine bridesmaids, wore my grandmother's dress and Chanel 'Vamp' on my nails. I walked down the aisle to 'All of My Love' by Led Zeppelin. Our vows were super-old-school Episcopalian—even though I'm not Episcopalian—I loved the idea of saying something that had been said over and over again like a mantra."

—KARYN STARR

"We ended our five-year engagement by booking the elephant enclosure for an Australian summer wedding at the Perth Zoo. I walked down the aisle on my own to Bob Dylan's 'I Want You,' carrying a bunch of sunflowers, and we ended the ceremony with June and Johnny Cash's 'Jackson.' I wore a vintage crochet minidress I'd bought for one hundred dollars! The Asian elephants a few feet behind us kept distracting me during the ceremony."

—SAYGAN KAHN

"We were married by a judge named Joan who also happened to be a surfer. She read passages from love letters that Rita Hayworth had written to Orson Welles. One of my nieces carried our daughter, Gigi, out—she was six months old, and she was sleeping. We wanted to have a plane fly over us with a banner that said, 'You may now kiss the bride,' but it was too stormy."

—BILL POWERS

## WANNA GET MARRIED ON A RUG? HERE'S HOW.

**On sand:** Try a flat woven rug. If you use a pile or a shag rug, it'll be impossible to get the sand out once the wedding is over. With a flat woven rug, the sand can be easily shaken off.

**On grass:** You'll want a heavier rug that'll help mat the grass down. Beware, though. Lumpy lightweight kilims + high heels = major tripping hazard.

**Don't forget:** Use a rug pad, even if your wedding is outdoors. And lay down your carpets right before the ceremony starts. You don't want wedding vendors rolling heavy machinery or carts over them.

# TYING THE KNOT TIGHT

Bottom line: there's something pretty magical (and not in a gag-me-Disney-Corp-heteronormative-patriarchal-princess-trope kind of way) about professing your love publicly to your partner. The two of you, eye to eye, hand in hand, in front of those who know you best. It's a once-in-a-lifetime experience, so make it count. But vows, albeit inherently beautiful in sentiment, can tend toward the vague and poetic, so why not take the radical step of really owning what it is you want to say and talking about what marriage truly means to you? We all get that you want to sleep in each other's arms every night and always find the time to play guitar beneath a tree, but don't forget about the real-deal-less-sexy-NOT-happily-ever-after-type-of-stuff that makes marriage really real. Why not publicly vow to always pay the bills on time? Or to sort through the recycling, wash the floors once a week, and look after your in-laws when they're too old to take care of themselves? How about saying, "I vow to work rigorously on our marriage, even in the toughest of times, and to accept that if we fall out of love down the line, we should commit to peacefully parting ways with respect and grace"?

An excerpt from *my* vows: "I will walk with you down the wide open road * from Big Sur to Siberia * from Greenland to Greenpoint * I will shade you from the sun and keep the dark days bright * I will laugh with you * I will let you be solitary * I will grow old with you * I will not leave you * I will treat your parents and siblings and family like my parents and siblings and family * I will make children with you * I will be faithful and peaceful and I will create with you a dazzling life rooted in beauty and edge and authenticity and integrity and God and pure raw truth * I will keep the refrigerator full for you, the bath scrubbed for you, and the bed warm for you * I will keep my heart clean for you * I will make your comfort my priority and your safety my ambition * I will give you all my love and I will be your home."

Then I took a deep breath and added, "I promise really, really, really, really, really hard to try to not read your emails."

# CHAPTER 9

# SEX, DRUGS + THE HORA

## SECRETS TO A STONE FOX CELEBRATION

'VE THROWN A LOT OF parties in my life and if there is one thing I pride myself on, it's being a good hostess. Granted, now that I have two kids, my idea of a party is kind of geriatric. I much prefer a 1970s-style hang to a wild rager. Think tons of crudite, Etta James, and floor pillows. I love events that encourage lazy hanging, engaging conversation, and mountains of delicious food. That's why I chose to make my wedding celebration a long and lazy Sunday afternoon meal modeled after my nana's famous lox-and-bagel brunch.

If that's not your style, then ignore me! There is no right way to celebrate. Regardless of whether you prefer the boozy blowout or the low-key backyard barbecue, the Stone Fox formula for throwing a great party is simple. Just follow these guidelines.

# EAT, DRINK, AND BE MARRIED
## ABUNDANCE IS KEY

Make sure there is plenty of food, no matter how small your budget is. Don't worry about making the food super fancy—as long as there is a lot of it, people will be happy. Maybe it's just the Jewish mother in me speaking, but I stand my ground here. Every minute your guests aren't fed is a minute that a bad vibe is generated. Serve hors d'oeuvres after the vows. I'm also a fan of a midnight snack, like milk and cookies or mini burgers and fries if you want your guests to party until the wee hours of the morn.

## LET THEIR CUPS RUNNETH OVER

Thirsty guests are cranky guests. But you don't have to break the bank with the booze and serve bougie cocktails. How about putting out water/lemonade/ice buckets of Bud Light on a table where guests can help themselves. A stacked bar is great, but so is serving only beer and/or wine. And if you can't afford to keep your guests drinking all night, shut down the party early and send them all to a nearby bar for after hours.

## FEEL THE LOVE

If there is one thing that all my clients tell me after their wedding, it's: "It all went by so fast—I wish I could have actually enjoyed the party!" If you're anything like me, you will probably get worried that people aren't having fun. One word of advice here: DON'T! You cannot control your guests' experience of your own wedding, but what you can do is lead by example. Eat, drink, dance. Do whatever you feel like doing. If you don't want to go around to every table and greet every guest and thank them for coming, then don't. Instead, at some point during the party, take the mic and sincerely thank everyone for coming.

## HAVE A RAIN PLAN

Think your mother-in-law is a schizophrenic beeyotch? She's nothing compared to the unpredictable nature of the weather. If you're having an outdoor wedding, make sure the tent is properly heated/properly cooled/durable enough to keep out heavy rain and mud. For a fall/winter wedding, keep a basket of blankets handy in case guests get cold. If it's heinously hot, leave paper fans at every place setting.

## FORGET THE FIRST DANCE . . .

. . . or any other traditional wedding "thing" that might not be *your* thing. I'm pretty open-minded, but the "first dance with Daddy" really puts a shiver down my spine. My dad and I are at our most comfortable at home, in his study, wearing sweats, eating hummus, and watching bad TV. Why in God's name would I want us to press our bodies together in an intimate waltz while other people watch? The same thing goes for tossing a bouquet over your shoulder, praying that it lands in the lap of your recently single college roommate, or shoving a piece of cake into your partner's face while smiling into a blinding kaleidoscope of flashbulbs. If you want to do these things, then by all means do them! But just because your mom is putting the pressure on you to do the hora doesn't mean it's mandatory.

## DON'T MAKE THEM DRIVE

Organize a customized Uber code, coordinate shuttles or a big yellow school bus back to the hotel. At the very least, have a car service on call.

## MINIMIZE MIC TIME

Sitting through hours of speeches featuring drunken private jokes from your childhood is truly a form of torture. Designate one of your besties who thrives at micromanagement to be the speech wrangler—and have them sort out logistics a few weeks before the wedding. There should only be a few speeches: the best man and maid of honor at the rehearsal dinner, Mom and Dad and a sibling (or two) during the party. And that's it.

## Mixologist Natasha David Believes in Beautiful Cocktails, Not Bud Light

**On His and Her Cocktails:** "It's really nice to have a drink for the bride and a drink for the groom. I always love a good champagne cocktail like a French 75. It's simple and delicious: gin, lemon juice, sugar, and sparkling wine. It's a versatile drink that your mother-in-law will love, and so will your best friend. You should also serve a drink that has a completely different flavor profile. Something for your grandfather who is used to drinking scotch on the rocks or bourbon. I love an old fashioned made with whiskey, sugar, and bitters. You can also change it up to accommodate the seasons. Make it with maple syrup for a fall wedding, or use rum in the summer."

**On Punch:** "Punches are a nice option because guests can help themselves. You want a good base spirit. Tequila is always great because it gets people in a fun, loose mood. Add another liquor to the tequila, some lemon or lime to brighten it up, and add seltzer for carbonation. Floating grapefruit peels and oranges on top look gorgeous and they'll also soak up some of the booze. Punch bowls usually come with small crystal punch glasses, which are ideal so people don't get too hammered. Keep in mind that your guests are going to be drinking a lot, so definitely keep the cocktails on the lower alcohol content side."

**On Sober Weddings:** "If the bride or groom doesn't drink, you can still absolutely serve beautiful cocktails. A simple syrup made by cooking ginger or strawberries and adding sugar can be divine if you add a little citrus and top it with seltzer water. It's way more special than just drinking a ginger ale."

**On Extra Special Touches:** "You don't need to overcomplicate the cocktail situation. Serve champagne when your guests arrive—it's such a treat. Make your cocktails with fresh ingredients— they will taste brighter if

you do so. I also recommend having a signature cocktail made specifically for your wedding. The great thing about a signature drink is that you can re-create it on your anniversary year after year and relive the magic."

# FOXY WEDDING GUEST ETIQUETTE FOR DUMMIES

*It's not your day, darling. Let's keep those martinis to a minimum.*

**DON'T Be That Girl**. Explosive emotional outbursts and/or tears, vomit, or urine due to excessive alcohol consumption is not a good look. Neither is doing coke in a bathroom stall while the groom's great-aunt Gertrude pees two feet away. A wedding is an adult rite of passage—don't behave like a fourteen-year-old.

**DON'T Be Slutty** . . . at the open bar, in the bathroom, in any public space, for that matter. I'm all for making out with the best man, but do it behind closed doors *after the party is over.*

**DON'T Start a Fight**. *Real Housewives*–style brawls are great entertainment, but only on Bravo. This is not the time to confront your ex-coworker who stole your pitch or snap at a former sorority sister for spilling wine on your dress.

**DON'T Go into the iPhone Zone.** Falling into a Facebook K-hole at the dinner table is rude (so is having your cellphone out on the table, period). If you need to check on the babysitter, excuse yourself and sneak outside. Also, no Instagram posts or pics unless you've been given the go-ahead by the couple.

**DON'T Complain.** Negative energy is a major no-no. If you catch yourself complaining about the fact that the food came out cold or the music is cheesy—stop. The bride and groom poured their hearts and bank accounts into this event in the hopes that you, dearest guest, would have a blast. If you don't like how things are being done, keep it to yourself.

**DON'T Forget to Say Thank You.** Before leaving, make sure you find the bride, groom, and each one of their parents. Take their hand, look them in the eye, and say: "Congratulations and thank you for hosting such a beautiful event." It might be a pain in the ass, but it's a classy gesture and well worth your time.

**DON'T Pour Your Heart Out to the Bride.** Feeling sentimental about the fact that your old friend, the bride, has just made the switch from single lady to walking the path of everlasting love? Don't take her hostage in the corner, and spend twenty minutes letting her know how much she means to you. The sentiment is sweet, but save it for when you debrief over brunch in a few weeks. This event is about her and him—NOT her and you.

## Organic Chef and Caterer Deena Chanowitz on Fresh Figs, Seasonal Food, and Crème Fraîche

**On the Farmers' Market:** "Design your menu around what's local and seasonal. Not only will it cost less, but it will taste better. The elegant design of the universe provides us exactly what our body needs when we need it. Beautiful purple basil is a gorgeous garnish, and looks and smells amazing in small vases and on charcuterie boards. I also like to carve rosettes out of lemon, lime, to-matoes, and beets. You can also pick up fruits and veggies to use as a display or as filler on platters. And garnishing any dish with edible pansy, rosebuds, chamomile, fresh figs, kumquats, or purple olives is always a good idea."

**On Nonalcoholic Mocktails:** "Use whatever fruit is in season: blueberries in summer, pomegranates in fall, citrus in winter. Muddle the fruit, add a splash of something acidic (fresh limes, lemons, or apple cider vinegar) and seltzer, then throw in some fresh herbs, chunks of fruit, and edible flowers."

**On Choosing a Caterer:** "Look at pictures and ask for referrals. Look for a caterer that creates seasonal fresh food that is beautifully presented. When I cater weddings, I ask the bride and groom what flavors they love and what kind of ambience they want to create. Then I design a menu that flows with the motif and venue."

**On Dips and Displays:** "I once did a party with all blue, indigo, and violet foods: wine grapes, blue cheese, purple cauliflower, pomegranates, figs, blue corn chips, and more. I made dips to complement the colors and flavors. It was gorgeous. One of my favorite spreads is roasted beets, horseradish, and crème fraîche with a drizzle of champagne vinegar. A great party trick is to create a lavish spread of seasonal veggies and then prep lots of dips to go along with it: ginger miso tahini, spicy plum sauce, feta harissa dip, chunky chimichurri style herb dip, or basil lemon sauce."

## Caterers Zahra Tangorra and Jennie Lupo on Pickle Towers, Purple Radishes, and Passed Hors D'oeuvres

**On Getting Guests to Eat:** "Catering should be all about creating a joyous experience. You want it to be easy and accessible. Passed hors d'oeuvres before the ceremony is a good way to ease the tension and get people in the mood to start nibbling. We love lasagna— it's the ultimate comfort food that everyone can share. Bring it out on a giant platter and have everyone get right in there. Other great dishes that are perfect for sharing include braised escarole, roasted potatoes, pork meatballs, and kale Caesar salad. Food served family style is always best. You don't have to worry about people eating at the same time or things getting cold."

**On Platters:** "We love bringing out large entrées on antique platters. A roast chicken looks way more appealing on a cool plate from the sixties or a mid-century modern tray. Experiment with placing unexpected things—like focaccia— on vintage cake stands. You can find beautiful ones in thrift stores or on eBay."

**On Abundance:** "We love towers. They draw people to the food. We like to glue vintage cake towers together and create gorgeous sculptural platters. Seafood towers are classic: head-on prawns, ceviche, a classic shrimp cocktail. The second layer can be oysters, the bottom can be strips of tuna and caviar. We also love a pickle tower. You can pickle anything—beets, string beans, eggs. Radishes are cheap and beautiful and fun to eat. Purple radishes and watermelon radishes go great with a yogurt-based green goddess dressing with lemon zest and herbs. Serve them with a tomato compound with cheese, lemon, and garlic."

# Bobbie Lloyd of Magnolia Bakery on How to Let Them Eat Cake

**On Choosing Your Sweets:** "You want the cake to represent who you are as a couple, but you don't want to take it too seriously. These days, about fifty percent of my clients want a vanilla cake. The other fifty percent varies. Lately everyone has been into the mixed multi-tiered cake—essentially three completely different cakes. For example, a bottom tier of carrot cake, a middle tier of chocolate, and a top tier of lemon cake with a meringue icing."

**On Fake Cake:** "It's not unusual for couples to want their cake to have a major wow factor. I worked with a couple who wanted a six-foot-tall cake, but they were only having about 150 people attend their wedding. So we made the bottom half Styrofoam covered in buttercream icing while the top half was actual cake."

**On Creative Cake Toppers:** "Cake toppers are a great way to let your personality as a couple shine through. I've seen everything from names spelled out in chocolate to felt dogs to otters. Once I designed a cake for a lingerie designer and a scientist—we topped it with a sculpture of them made from bones enclosed in a glass case."

**On Alternatives to Wedding Cakes:** "Your nationality and cultural history can influence what kind of dessert you want at your wedding. My husband is Italian so we had a huge traditional Italian cookie table. I've also done weddings that have beautiful tables of nuts and baklava, or pecan pie. Sometimes clients will have a separate smaller cake made, or make the top tier of their multi-tiered cake gluten free."

**On Cutting Out Tradition:** "Ask your baker to make a small version of your wedding cake on your first anniversary. It's a more elegant option than keeping a slice in your freezer for a year."

## Caroline Connolly, Lead Singer of
## The Lovebullies, on Green Rooms, Grub,
## and Full-Tilt Boogie

**On How to Choose a Band:** "When the band strikes their first chord, it should have broad appeal to everyone in the room! You know your tastes and those of your family and friends, so select a band that can follow suit. A good way to see if you like their vibe is to meet them at a performance before the wedding. Hang with them between sets and talk about music. Make sure you're really hip to each other's vibe. You want this to be a perfect match."

**On Green Rooms and Grub:** "Depending on the venue, there may already be a PA (sound system with speakers, mics, monitors, lights, etc.). If not, that needs to be worked out in advance. A member of the band should always scout out the venue before the big day. Make sure you are insanely clear about access, power availability, tents, and weather protection if you are outdoors. All bands need a green room or hangout space with a bathroom, water and snacks. Also, make sure you factor in the band when giving your caterers a head count. We need to eat!"

**On DJs and Live Bands:** "A DJ is a programmable human that will play whatever you ask for in an orderly predictable fashion. A live band is a sweaty, writhing mass of sexy humanity sporting miniskirts, go-go boots, and large hairdos, baring their souls and windpipes for an evening of rock mayhem, shenanigans, and orgasmic guitar solos."

**On the Playlist:** "Everyone loves Amy Winehouse's 'Rehab,' 'I Love You Baby' by Frank Sinatra, 'Venus' by Bananarama, 'These Boots Are Made for Walking' by Nancy Sinatra, 'Blue Moon' by The Marcels, 'Preacher Man' by Dusty Springfield, 'Ode to Billie Joe' by Bobbie Gentry, and 'Me and Bobby McGee' by Janis Joplin. Whatever happens, the band should never play 'D-I-V-O-R-C-E' by Tammy Wynette."

## DJ Colleen Crumbcake, Founder of Sugartown Industries, on How to Keep That Dance Floor Full

**On Choosing a DJ:** "The best DJs are the ones you've heard at other people's weddings and loved, or who come recommended by multiple people you trust. Check out what you can about them online at a reputable wedding site (I would recommend this over Yelp) and meet with them before making a final decision. Things to look for are: someone who listens to you and gets what you are saying, someone

who can give you suggestions regarding flow and music, and someone who has experience doing weddings. A club DJ is not necessarily going to be a great wedding DJ—weddings are an entirely different beast. A lot of people want to listen to online mixes but it's not the best way to find a wedding DJ. Often it will demonstrate how great their mixing skills are, but it won't tell you much about what they would play at your wedding."

**On Equipment:** "A DJ should bring a mixer, a laptop (and turntables if that's what they spin with), two power speakers, two speaker stands, one handheld wireless microphone, and all cabling needed for their setup. They might also bring a subwoofer, a mic stand, and a corded microphone as a backup. The client should expect to have a six-foot table covered with a tablecloth available for the DJ that's close to a power source. They should also expect the DJ to eat a meal during the night."

**On Why to Choose a DJ Over a Band:** "Bands are great, but super expensive. Even an excellent band can sound like really great karaoke after a while. DJs can change things quickly if they find themselves in unpopular territory. A band is generally at the mercy of a set list."

**On Collaborating with a Couple:** "I usually meet with the bride and groom twice before the wedding. Once to decide if they want to work with me and a final meeting closer to the date of the wedding. At the final meeting, I review their important songs (first dance, parent dances, etc.) and any songs they want me to try to squeeze in throughout the night. I want them to feel like I understand what they want and don't want when they hand me the keys for the night—and that I can throw in some surprises. Once a couple insisted I play '99 Problems' and the older people all stopped, stunned, in the middle of the dance floor and stared at me slack-jawed. I quickly threw on Young MC's 'Bust a Move' to save that disaster."

**On Playing to the Crowd:** "The goal is to keep the dance floor full. It can get extremely challenging when I'm working with a couple that's very strict about the songs they want played during the dance set and the crowd is not responding well to them. Even your cool friends want to hear those ridiculous, nostalgic, sing-along songs. I would also recommend a smaller dance floor. A smaller dance floor is a better dance floor—people feel less self-conscious and will be out there all night without worrying that others are watching them."

**On Foolproof Songs:** Stevie Wonder's "Sir Duke" or "Signed, Sealed, Delivered I'm Yours"; Frank Sinatra's "The Way You Look Tonight"; Michael Jackson's "Rock with You"; Al Green's "Let's Stay Together"; Beyoncé's "Love on Top"; Four Tops' "Ain't No Woman"; Frankie Valli's "Can't Take My Eyes Off You"; Dion's "The Wanderer"; Drake's "Hold On, We're Going Home."

**On Foxy First Dance Songs:** The Magnetic Fields' "It's Only Time"; Neil Young's "Harvest Moon"; The Flamingos' "I Only Have Eyes for You"; Ramones' "Baby, I Love You"; Neutral Milk Hotel's "In the Aeroplane Over the Sea"; Otis Redding's "That's How Strong My Love Is"; Cat Power's "Sea of Love"; Stevie Wonder's "As"; Sam Cooke's "You Send Me"; Leon Bridges's "Coming Home"; Sinéad O'Connor's "You Do Something to Me"; The Zombies' "This Will Be Our Year."

# GIRLS ON FILM

*Fashion and Wedding Photographer Josie Miner on the Importance of Being Compatible with the Person Behind the Camera*

"I always recommend meeting with your potential photographer over coffee to get a feel for their disposition. You want to work with someone whose energy and

aesthetic you jibe with. I'm more interested in making photographs that feel true to the spirit of the wedding than following a shot list, for example. So if I meet with a client who wants super high-def, heavily posed, and retouched pictures, I'll try to refer them to a colleague who can accommodate their vision. Your photographer should make you feel at ease from the start. You're going to be spending a lot of time with this person. You want someone who will keep things light, festive, and fun, and who can sensitively navigate family dynamics and de-escalate potentially stressful moments."

# IS WEDDING SEX ESSENTIAL?

Absolutely. And if you don't have mind-blowingly intimate intercourse while staring into each other's eyes on a bed of red rose petals while breaking your virginal hymen, your marriage will be doomed from the start. In the canon of urban legends, I can't decide which one is the more bogus: that there are alligators in the sewers of New York City or that every newly married bride and groom fuck each other's brains out post-party. Let's just say, I've heard it all: couples who have gotten so wasted that they've puked and passed out, couples who've ordered room service in sweatpants and watched Adam Sandler movies, couples who've gotten halfway to home base only to come face-to-face with their partner's deflated drunk dick. If *doing it* is important to you, the first thing to do is let go of the fantasy. It. Might. Not. Happen. The same deal applies to sex on your honeymoon—I speak from experience on that one.

*♡♡♡*

# ONE COUPLE, ONE PARTY, ONE CHANCE. ALL THEY WANTED TO DO WAS DANCE.

## AFTER MOM AND DAD WENT HOME . . . THESE FOUR COUPLES GOT DOWN AND DIRTY.

"There were so many crazy, special moments. But one in particular that stands out was walking into the teepee at four a.m. to find a group of ten friends in the midst of a full-blown jam session–tribal dance party."

—SOPHIE GREEN

"My chief concern regarding my dress was that I could dance in it. I actually changed into Nike Dunks to really get down, and Wes switched into some sick white party pants after the ceremony. We danced our faces off in a mirrored and marble-filled ballroom. The closest thing to euphoria I have ever felt was dancing with Wes to LCD Sound-system's 'Dance Yourself Clean.' The dance party ended

at one a.m. and twenty to thirty people went back to our suite and stayed until four a.m., when the hotel said it was bedtime. And it was."

—CHRISTINA DEVAUX

"Our friend Ethan deejayed and the three of us promised each other that we'd kick off the jams in a serious way—we wanted a *Soul Train* wedding—that was the mission. The music was incredible—tons of funk, r&b, and soul—and everyone completely got down. At one point all the glass windows in the restaurant were fogged up. The dancing was the main event at our wedding. I remember everyone staying 'til around midnight. Then we went back to the motel where all our friends were and sat outside with them, smoked joints, and howled into the moonlight."

— SUSAN KAPLOW

"I was seven and a half months pregnant—I danced so hard that I had to rest until I gave birth."

— JAMIE ROSENTHAL

# THE ELEGANT EXIT

THESE COUPLES GOT AWAY WITHOUT
EVER PUTTING PEDAL TO METAL.

**Francesca Choy-Kee:** "After our wedding at a little Italian restaurant in Brooklyn, we walked home through the neighborhood to our apartment rental hand in hand, with a 'Just Married' garland pinned to our backs."

**Samantha Bowles:** "We had a sunrise ceremony on the beautiful beaches of Lanikai in Hawaii, and didn't plan anything for the ride home. But after we said our vows, a pedicab covered in 'Just Married' shaving cream and tin cans surprised us outside— then biked us all through town. People came out of their homes and screamed as we passed by."

**Lindsay Vint:** "We got married at City Hall in full Western regalia, then walked over the Brooklyn Bridge."

**Jessica Shortall:** "After our ceremony in the church chapel of Oxford, I changed out of my wine red heels into black Camper flats, and we walked on cobblestones in the rain."

# CHAPTER 10

# FREE TO BE
# YOU AND ME

## TWO HEARTS, ONE HOME,
## NOW WHAT . . . WTF ?

Finish
Thank you
cards.

## START FROM SCRATCH

THE WEDDING'S OVER. WELL DONE. Before you start berating yourself for all the things you wish you'd done differently, take a minute to acknowledge all your hard work. You threw a kickass party and are still alive to tell the tale. Your mother-in-law is back in her city of origin, flashing pics of your first dance to strangers on her flip phone. Your flower crown is drying on the shelf, you've made waffles and paninis and smoothies in your new blender, and you're procrastinating from writing thank-you notes. Now you can return to regular programming.

Every Nancy Meyers movie out there would have you believe that newlywed bliss is a cozy montage of pillow fights, sparring playfully with chopsticks over the last egg roll, and impromptu dance-parties-turned-steamy-sex-sessions.

Um, no.

A wedding is one thing. Marriage, however, is an entirely different animal. A wedding is a shiny kaleidoscope full of unicorns and fairies designed to warm hearts and razzle-dazzle even the most dead-eyed cynics. Marriage is the total opposite. A plodding, responsible journey, with no endgame in sight, it's rooted in safety, security, and the promise of forever. There are no fireworks or red getaway cars. Once you're in it, you're in it. For good.

I started this book by saying that before I met M I was an existential mess with crippling sciatica on Prozac. Now, nine years later, I am wondrously reborn. I'm never sad, never sick, never fraught. I am complete.

Just kidding.

I am still an existential mess with crippling sciatica on Prozac. Plagued by a constant, nagging sensation that, somehow, no matter what kind of success I achieve, I am a failure at heart. Not smart enough, skinny enough, blond enough, blah blah blah. Lots of mornings I wake up and want to crawl back down under the covers. I still feel lonely on my birthday. I still stare at Instagram and think that everyone is at the party but me.

Marriage has not made me complete. It has not taken away the ache. But it teaches me, day by day, how to stay. To stay strong and calm. To stay put, despite the pain. Some days, marriage is like lying on a pink sand beach; others, it's like being trapped in a box with no air. Sex, family, union, home, money, growth—it's all so massive, so mind-blowing, so bizarre. But the more raw, honest love I invest in all of it, the more raw honest love I receive. I guess that's what makes it all worthwhile.

# HONEYMOON'S OVER: NOW WHAT?

## TWELVE TIPS FOR SURVIVING THE FIRST YEAR OF MARRIAGE WITHOUT GOING INSANE

### SOLO BATHROOM TIME IS ESSENTIAL

Nicole Kidman may look tremendously sexy when she pees in front of Tom Cruise in *Eyes Wide Shut,* but I don't recommend trying it in real life. I know it can be really tempting to treat your husband like your BF roommate and be all: "Babe, come here and brush your teeth while I take out my tampon," but trust me when I say that nothing good can come from it. Please maintain privacy around bodily functions; i.e.: poo with the door closed.

### HAVE SEX

Do it, even when you're not in the mood. At least two to three times a week is ideal, but never less than once. Regular sex will keep you connected on a cosmic and cellular level. And every once in a while, put on sexy clothes and go to a fun party. Constant sweat-suit-clad homebody husband and wife does not a steamy passionate sex life make.

### PICK A STANCE ON PORN

Decide your collective position on porn and masturbation and stick to it. I know it's an awkward talk to have, but doing damage control preemptively will save you a lot of drama in the long run. Every single woman I know has to deal with this one—Internet porn is a reality, and most likely one or both of you watch it. If porn and/or masturbation is making it hard for either of you to have an orgasm or to connect with each other in bed, then it's officially a problem and should be addressed in couples therapy ASAP.

## DO DATE NIGHT

Shave your legs, make a reservation at a chic bistro, get tickets to a play or movie, hit an art opening, paint the town. It will electrify your vibe and spark up sexy memories from your courtship phase.

## IT'S ALL IN THE DETAILS

The moments of connection don't have to be profound, but they do have to be, period. Whether it's staying in bed for an extra five minutes to drink coffee and cuddle, walking to the subway holding hands, or throwing his clothes in the laundry bag when you're headed out to wash a load, small, thoughtful gestures speak volumes.

## CELEBRATE THE MILESTONES

Holidays and anniversaries don't all have to be about red roses and five-star restaurants, but they should be acknowledged. Sort out where you stand on gifts, too. Are they important to you? To him? If so, make it a thing. Marking the passage of time together is vital. This whole marriage thing is a crazy long journey—taking a break every few miles to refuel and reflect is paramount.

## A COUPLE THAT SNOOZES TOGETHER . . .

Try to go to sleep at the same time every night. Take an extra twenty minutes to snuggle, read, and talk before you turn out the light.

## DON'T SNOOP

Believe me, I know how tempting it is. You open his computer to order Seamless and end up poking around his Gmail account and search History just for the helluvit. Word to the wise: Don't do it. If you have reason to be suspicious, get yourselves to couples therapy where you can talk about your fears with another person present.

## ENCOURAGE GUY TIME

Don't hijack your husband's free time—give him space to both make and maintain new and old friendships. For M's birthday last year I gave him two hundred dollars in cash and made a reservation at a steakhouse for him and two friends. Your partner's life shouldn't revolve around meeting your needs.

## CALL HIS PARENTS

I know it can seem taxing to even find the time to call your own family, but please don't neglect his in the process! They are now your family, too. Every week take a selfie of the two of you, or a pretty pic of your apartment, and send it out with a quick text note: *Thinking of both of you and sending lots of love.* Done.

SNAPPED THIS PIC OF MY NANA AND GRANDPA,
MID-MAKEOUT, IN MICHIGAN, 1998

## DINNER PARTIES

Whenever M and I have a dinner party it gives us the extra push we needed to hang the curtains, fix the dishwasher, clean the carpet, and dust those linty corners that we've been meaning to get to for months. Light the candles, cook all day, fill the vases with flowers. It's really gratifying to get a bunch of your loved ones in one room and see how full your life (and home!) is together.

## INFIDELITY DOESN'T MEAN THE END

Hard truth here: He might, you might, it happens and it doesn't have to be a dealbreaker. The spoken vows are lovely, but afterward, life can get messy. Lots of my friends have dealt with infidelity in their marriages and are still together to tell the tale. It's symptomatic of other issues, and if you and your partner have the courage to tackle them together, you can emerge on the other side stronger than ever.

## Professional Organizer Laura Cattano on Sex Toys, Sofas, and Sentimental Items

**On Cohabitation:** "Your home should reflect what's important to you. Before you move in with your partner, you should both create a list of how you want to live. Is cooking important? Is having a proper dining table? A desk? Or is a laptop on a chair good enough? Do you like to entertain? Dinner parties, watching the game, cocktail parties? Do you need a space to meditate and pray? A comfortable reading spot? You should also think about how you want each room to

feel. Do you like a calming space or do you need to be energized? Is color important? Lots of family photos or art? Or do you prefer a minimalist aesthetic? Once your lists are complete, compare. You will have some overlapping needs — and when you don't agree, don't compromise. I once commented on a client's sofa and they responded that neither of them liked it, but it was the only one they could agree on. I thought that was depressing. It's important that you each get 'wins.' For instance, you can pick the sofa if your partner gets to pick the wall color. This way, no one feels slighted. Just because you're a couple doesn't mean you're not still your own person.

"A balance of open and closed storage is key. Some things don't need to be seen: pills, sex toys, glasses, and tissues. That's what closed nightstands with drawers are for. No one wants to see office supplies, chargers, extra totes, and old mail. Think drawers, cabinets, and boxes are for the crap. And Muji bins are your best friend. So is The Container Store."

**On Merging Belongings:** "The most important thing is respecting each other's things. George Carlin said it best: 'Have you ever noticed that their stuff is shit and your shit is stuff?' So true . . . that's why it's best to deal with your stuff before talking to your partner about theirs. It's also why it's so important that you each have a space that you can do with what you please. Even if it's just a room or a closet. I worked with a newlywed couple who was expecting a baby and she wanted to throw out all his baseball caps and Grateful Dead paraphernalia but he wanted to hang on to them. So we organized all of his beloved belongings in bins on the top of his closet where she couldn't see them but he could still enjoy them. He needed to hold on to the relics of his past life. You don't have to lose your personal identity just because you're becoming a dad!"

**On the Mission of Your Home:** "Come up with three words and make them your mission statement. For example, my three words are 'simple, modern, and elegant.' I try to relate everything I take into my life to those words—even my pens, my bracelets, my sweaters. Otherwise you're filling your life with stuff that doesn't inspire you."

**On the Burden of Stuff:** "You carry a mental inventory of everything you own with you everywhere you go. It ends up being a huge burden, even when it's not surrounding you physically. My motto is: 'It's not about having a lot of stuff, it's about having the *right* stuff.' The *right* stuff adds to your life. And if something isn't adding to your life, it's directly taking away from it."

**On Sentimental Items:** "I get asked a lot about sentimental items. They serve a purpose as long as they evoke a positive memory. There is so much negativity coming at us as soon as we leave the house: traffic, a crowded subway, an unappreciative boss or customers, bad weather, etc. It's so important to keep our home free of bad energy. Sometimes you need to let go of the past to make room for positivity. Toss images or cards that have lost their meaning. Don't save something because you think you're 'supposed' to. For larger things that take up too much room, consider taking pictures of them and making a photo book. A client once begged me to get her husband to toss his collection of printed T-shirts he'd

collected over the years. After I kicked her out of the room to discuss this with him alone, he told me the images on the shirts were the important part and agreed to take photos of each. We made a little assembly line and did it right there. Everyone won."

## Therapist and Financial Wellness Expert Amanda Clayman on Debt, Compromise, and Communication

**On Starting the Conversation:** "Money comes up all the time when you're dating. A good way to talk about budget and income is by offering to treat them. Or say 'Thanks for the four-star restaurant, but I would love to go bowling the next time.' It's awkward to bring it up, but it's better in the long run. Once you start getting more serious, you can have the harder talks about student debt, credit card debt, and your income. Talk about it in a general sense: The goal is to get the bullet points of the other person's financial life. You want to suss out your own comfort level and how honest the communication is. No one is financially perfect. Most couples come from different financial backgrounds. One person is usually more risk averse than another. One person might want to invest in foreign markets or new tech companies. One might be into solid dividends, blue chips, and bonds. There is no road map here. We all come to relationships with our distortions when it comes to money."

**On Debt:** "Debt doesn't have to be a dealbreaker. But it is a red flag if someone is totally unconcerned about it. Be open though—people evolve over the course of a long-term relationship. You can say: 'I was raised that credit card debt was a no-no—what was your family's take on it?' If you start to disclose your feelings, you can find some room to work together. As the relationship gets more serious, you eventually want to have the conversation about your long-term finances. Talk about where you land on kids and college. Do you want your kids to pay for college so it will make them more responsible? Do you want to start saving for it now? All of this is necessary information. The thing about these conversations is that you can't just have them once. You have to discuss them again and again. You don't want to only talk about money when something is wrong. A big part of adulting is taking care of your finances. And the goal is for your partner to understand your point of view, not to argue them into a corner and prove that they're wrong."

**On Paying for the Wedding:** "Forget tradition. Talk about what's important to you. Keep the conversation focused on 'I.' You're not a bum if you can't pay for it or a gold digger if you want help. It's an awkward, uncomfortable conversation—stay with it! A lot of couples elect to pay for the wedding themselves because they don't want to deal with their parents' expectations."

**On Joint Finances:** "There are three ways to organize your money. The first is that all the income goes into the same pot—and all the expenses are paid out of that pot. It's both the individual pot and the joint pot. If there are significant differences in income, this requires a higher degree of coordination. The problem is, if one person spends all the money, the other person might not know it, and the account can get overdrawn. It can also get competitive. Like 'I have to spend the money before my spouse spends it.' The second way to handle your finances is to make everything largely separate. You divide the expenses. One person takes electric and phone bills; one person takes the rent. This allows for the highest degree of independence so that you don't have to talk about everything, but you do have to closely coordinate your joint goals. The third option is to keep everything separate. A lot of people do this to avoid having the hard conversations. Then the baby comes along and it's like: 'Who does the baby belong to financially?' It really highlights the shortcomings of this organizational system."

**On Savings:** "It's important to sit down on a monthly basis and look at your accounts. The two of you should look at your income and what you are spending. Usually one partner is much more anxious about money than the other. Anxious spenders hate to see money go. It makes them feel unsafe. Often they partner with someone who is more free with money. You don't have to count pennies every day, but you do have to sit down on a monthly basis and review what's there. Look to your partner as a resource—not as a boss."

**On a Healthy Financial System:** "A healthy system is one where both people are participating. It's equal, flexible, and sustainable. It can change over time according to circumstances. Sometimes one person takes the lead, then they get a new job, and the other person can take over. It shouldn't be so hard that you're gritting your teeth to get it done. Joint finances should be transparent. No secrets. Even if you are very independent, the other person has a right to know what's going on. Talk about your values. Communicate. Be a good listener. Be concrete. Negotiate. Compromise. Remember: It's not about getting your way. You want to keep your system happy and functional."

## Psychotherapist and Relationship Expert Esther Perel on Comfort Food, Apple Products, and the Secret to Long-Term Sex

**On Marriage:** "Fifty percent of marriages end in divorce—and yet, despite our knowledge, we continue to take the leap of faith again and again. If you knew that fifty percent of the Apple products you bought would break, would you buy them? Marriage is the most loaded enterprise we engage in. We want belonging, grounding, and a secure attachment. We want continuity and predictability and dependability, but at the same time we want novelty and surprise and expansion. Marriage is a choice—and with every choice comes inherent loss. We want to find ourselves through our partner, but we simply cannot. Every mythic story, from *Ulysses* on, is written about home and journey. You don't find yourself at home. You have to take the journey."

**On Once the Wedding Is Over:** "After a while reality kicks in. The romantic ideal dissolves. You realize that the person you chose is not a figment of your imagination. And you're no longer in the idyllic Eden state. Your partner stops validating you all the time. Your insecurities start acting up."

**On Sex and Romance:** "Married couples stop having sex because they apply this pragmatic model to it. At the end of the day, most couples sit on the couch, watch TV, and then stroke their partner's arm to get them wet. Then they move to the bedroom and say: 'Do you want to do it'? Think about it: all day you're at work, charming everyone you come into contact with, flirting with strangers. Then the second you walk into your home, you put on a pair of discolored sweatpants. This is not sexy! Try doing the reverse for a change. Meet your partner for lunch when you are awake and engaged. This is foreplay. Stay home for breakfast once in a while, bring your kids to school, then meet back at the house. Feel free from responsibility and accountability. It will make you playful and generative and full of possibility—these are the essential erotic ingredients. I also like sexting. It keeps the mystery alive. Knowing our partner is essential to establishing emotional safety—but desire requires elements of the unknown. That's where romance lives; it's sex with a plot. The plot is about the state of waiting to be chosen."

**On Passion:** "If you want truly passionate sex, you have to have a lot of maintenance sex. It's like food. You eat a lot of regular meals, but every now and then you have a really special one. You can't always have a five-star meal or you would starve. Comfort food is so important; so is cozy, warm sex. The problem is that married sex becomes this goal-oriented, performance-oriented, genitally-oriented activity. Couples treat it like a five-minute drive-by with two-minute foreplay. They stop kissing. It's so important to pay attention to all the nooks and crannies of the body. To give touch and take touch. Making love is a unique experience in which, for a moment, you are separate and together at the same time. You are penetrated without feeling like you are going to be swallowed up. It's one of the most powerful kinds of intimacy."

# LOVE IS ALL IN THE DETAILS

*Three Foxes on the little things that make a big difference*

## ROUTINE

"On weekdays, I practice the art of not checking emails right away. Instead, I have coffee in bed with my husband at six-fifteen, then we take the dog for a walk. Sometimes I get in the car and pretend I'm from the suburbs and go grocery shopping in New Jersey. My husband finds my job fascinating; he loves the fact that it's always a chess game, a total roller coaster. Even though we have our independent lives, I fill him in on what's going on in my day-to-day. It's really important to have people in your life who can ride the highs and lows with you. I think my view of love is very much about the day in and day out. That's where love shines—in the daily routine."

—BECCA THORPE

## COUPLES THERAPY

"Being two different people in two different places in life is the greatest challenge of our marriage. With couples therapy, I get to see that his intentions are to love me and to be a good person. Most of our time together is about the kids and dishes and work—it can be hard to remember what made us fall in love."

—LATONYA YVETTE

## MONEY TALKS

"Money is not a source of conflict. We each keep our own personal bank accounts, but we share with one another. I earn the primary income. She's doing her PhD and working for a nonprofit. It's not fifty-fifty. She deals with organizing and logistics around bills and I actually pay them. That's how we stay organized. She can pick up where my weaknesses are."

—NICOLETTE MASON

# AFTER "I DO"

## LOVE STORIES FROM THE FRONT LINES

### Lesley Arfin, Married to Paul for One Year

**On Planning a Wedding:** "The experience of planning a wedding, of making a legally binding commitment in front of our family and friends, made us closer. Our finances changed. We made a will together and came up with an estate plan. It wasn't intense, it was actually lovely and fun to think of our future together."

**On Sex:** "Sex is always a hard subject to tackle, but we don't put a lot of pressure on each other to do what we've heard people say is 'normal.' For example, if a 'normal' sex life means having sex twice a week, then I guess our sex life is 'not normal.' That's bullshit. We don't count, we don't keep checks and balances on anything, especially not our sex life. I couldn't tell you the quantity of our lovemaking, but I can tell you that when we do it, we love it. Well, I'll speak for myself. I love it. And I certainly don't compare it with the sex lives of other married people, but let's assume everyone is a lot more alike than not. Who the fuck wants to have sex twice a week?"

**On Being at Home:** "We love to sit in our living room and watch a movie. Paul will sit in the Eames chair cuddling with the dog, and I'll sit at the table and paint or draw or do needlepoint. It takes us forever to pick out something we can both agree on. Paul likes action movies and psychological thrillers, and I'm like: 'Let's watch *Sisters*!' Sometimes I'll snuggle up in the chair with him and our goldendoodle, Judy."

## Lisa Lundy, Married to Brook for Five Years

**On Their Courtship:** "We were friends for five years before we got married. On my thirty-fifth birthday we went out for bad sushi and had a nervous talk about trying to date. Then we kissed outside the restaurant."

**On the First Year of Marriage:** "It was really hard trying to integrate the fantasy of what I thought it was going to be with

the reality of it all. Plus, we decided to start trying to have a baby before we got engaged, which put extra pressure on us from the start. Only we couldn't get pregnant. So our whole sex life turned into this timed, mechanical thing. We had to have sex every other day starting on the sixth day of my cycle. There was no romance in it. No desire. Nothing hot about it at all. All my friends were getting pregnant left and right, and I was going to the fertility clinic all the time, getting acupuncture, eating a certain way. But no matter what I did, month after month, the pregnancy test kept coming out negative. And I kept thinking he was going to leave me for some young, fertile chick."

**On Acceptance:** "Years went by. I did tons of IVF. Brook had to give me the shots. He's now basically a registered nurse. He had to comfort me and listen to me and let me rage. It took a toll on him, too. Eventually I wasn't the only one crying. We had to become a team. Fertility stuff could have become divisive and sent us in opposite directions, but instead it made us closer. And finally, after some very extreme measures, it worked. I got pregnant. I had never seen a positive pregnancy test in my life. We were beyond speechless."

**On Becoming Parents:** "These days, we're focused on our two little boys, but we still maintain a strong sense of 'us.' There's a new level of vulnerability and intimacy between us now, this unspoken belief that we're in it, no matter what, for the long haul. You don't want to have just a great sexy lover as your partner in life—you want a friend. Brook is the person I always want to be around. He makes everything better."

## Alexa Wilding, Married to Ian for Six Years

**On Their Courtship**: "We worked at the same gallery. The first time I saw him he was standing on a ladder with tattoos and a white tank top and a measuring tape attached to his belt. We saw a movie on our first date, then went for spaghetti and meatballs."

**On the First Year of Marriage:** "It was really rocky. I quit my job at the gallery to focus on music but I wasn't bringing in any money. I felt so guilty that I would take jobs I didn't want, then quit to go on tour. I had seen my own parents' marriage fall apart because my mom worked all the time instead of tending to her creative self, and I didn't want to make that mistake. Then I got pregnant and we thought the new baby was going to fix everything, but then I miscarried at twelve weeks. It took two months of mourning the loss of the baby to realize how much we wanted a family. During Hurricane Sandy we double-wished on a chicken bone, had sex, then found out I was pregnant again with twins."

**On Having a Sick Kid:** "On my son Lou's first birthday we found out that he had a brain tumor. He had to have emergency surgery, then six months of chemotherapy. One week in the hospital, one week out. We alternated nights so one parent was always at home with our other son, West. Ian and I only saw each other after one of us had been in the hospital for twenty-four hours without sleeping. But we kept the romance alive by texting sweet messages all day long, then we'd have sex quickly before the other person left for the hospital, even though sex was the last thing on our minds."

**On Reintegration:** "After chemo was over and Lou's hair grew back, we got the boys matching buzz cuts. We're all learning how to be a family again, enjoying the small things like waking up on Sunday and making pancakes and looking at dinosaurs at the Natural History Museum. Last week the boys were standing under the big whale, screaming that the sky was falling down, and Ian and I looked at each other and whispered, 'But it didn't.'"

## Meredith Pugh, Married to Jeff for Twelve Years

**On Their Courtship:** "Jeff was not someone I had my sights on. I knew him through mutual friends and he seemed like a drama queen, full of problems and noise and stewing. Still, he's very good-looking, and there's an edge of distance and anger to his persona that's very sexy. I saw him out in the neighborhood one day and told him I had a date with some douchebag that night. I asked him how I should wear my hair. He said, 'If I had a

date with you, I wouldn't care how you wore your hair.' The next time I saw him, he asked me out. On our first date he rolled up in a Chevy Cavalier with a single peony. Turns out he was incredibly poetic, really looking for true love. He completely took me by surprise."

**On Chemistry:** "We're a chemically true couple. There's a completely unstated, unidentifiable, no-language-to-describe the pheromone-like chemistry that can happen between people. It can happen without words. No matter what kinds of problems we have, or what struggles, there is always a connection between us."

**On Sex:** "Once the baby came, there was so much pressure and exhaustion. As a culture, we're not very transparent about how hard having kids is on the marriage. The relationship you had in the past is gone. Suddenly there's a new human in the house that requires all this care. Couplehood and parenthood are not the same. Plus, we had opposite schedules. He was a bartender, and I worked in advertising. The sleep deprivation and resentment started to impact us, and we just couldn't find the time to have sex. It would take a lot of pressure off couples during the early parenthood years if they could just accept that sex is not a huge priority—and that it doesn't mean the marriage is fucked. We've gone long periods of time without sex, and it's taken us a long time to find our way back to sexual intimacy. These days, we always have sex in the bathroom at every big party we go to. It's fun and unexpected and hot. We go to more parties in summer, so we have more sex in the summer."

**On What the Future Holds:** "I see us at seventy-five having a whole other marriage focused around our minds and our home. By then, we'll be past all the logistical, practical angst of the parenting years, and more into the mystery of life. We'll be exploring, creating, seeing the world."

## Tara Averill, Married to Craig
## for Nine Years + Divorced Four

**On Their Courtship:** "I met my former husband when I was on a date at Coney Island with another guy. It was a group date with friends. We got along so well that day. I was on an obsessive diet and he was looking to lose a few pounds. That's how we bonded. He asked the guy I was with if it was okay if he asked me to dinner. We went to dinner. We had both spent our early twenties partying really hard in the East Village, we were ready to settle down and be healthy. Fast-forward three years . . . we were married."

**On Consciously Uncoupling:** "This may not sound flowery, but for deeply personal reasons our arrangement as a married couple stopped working. It was heartbreaking. We worked very hard individually to maintain a healthy, sane relationship so that our children felt secure. We were very clear, and had a practical plan about how it was going to work. We took suggestions from experts in the field. We divided our time with them fifty-fifty. We put a calendar in each house so the kids would know where they had to be at all times. Divorce brings so much unknown into kids' lives so we worked hard to maintain stability and consistency so they felt very secure. It's really important to understand that the marital relationship is its own dynamic, and then there is the family. I think people confuse the two. Just because you don't want to be in an intimate romantic relationship with someone anymore, doesn't mean that you don't love them, enjoy your family life together, and make great parenting partners."

**On What It's Like Now:** "Our co-parenting relationship is solid. We are very bonded by the love we have for the children—and I've experienced a more expanded definition of love as a result of this process. Love is so much more than romance. I recently met his girlfriend, who is lovely. The whole thing is a lesson in loving and acceptance. In some ways this can be better preparation for our kids than the Beaver Cleaver family. Resilience, open-mindedness, the ability to change—these are powerful skills for life."

**On Christmas:** "His father is handicapped, and I live in an elevator building, so we do the holidays at my apartment. Last Christmas, his dad came to my house with my mom and our kids and it was great. We were all in our PJs opening presents, drinking coffee, and listening to reggae Christmas songs. Afterward we went out for Chinese food. I feel so lucky to have this beautiful family."

## Ellen Rosen, Married to Robert for Forty-Five Years

MY PARENTS

**On Their Courtship:** "We first met when I was in graduate school and on a date with his brother. I thought Robert was beautiful, intellectually sharp, and very curious. He seemed solid and grounded. Plus, we shared a love of ancient Greek sculpture and archaeology. I liked that he made himself chicken for dinner, that he had a good job. I was eating frozen foods every night. I fancied myself a freewheeling bohemian. I grew up in a very old-fashioned, traditional, patriarchal environment. My dad was a personal injury trial lawyer; my mom was a housewife. She took care of the kids and his needs. He had a very volatile temper."

**On the Challenges of Marriage:** "Many marriages of our generation were fashioned around keeping our husbands happy so that there was calm in the house. Whenever Robert came home, I made sure the house was orderly and there was dinner on the table. Everything was very chaotic in the early years. We had three kids, dogs, cat, the doorbell was always ringing. A child always needed to be driven to gymnastics or soccer or a math tutor. I worked some, but my main priority was ensuring that Robert was happy. It was stressful."

**On Rituals:** "I learned how important it is to have routines as a family. Friday night, we'd eat in the dining room and light candles and read poems. We had the grandparents over for dinner twice a week. We had a date night every Wednesday. The family sat down for dinner together every night at six-thirty, and we'd go around the table and tell one good thing about the day and one bad thing. It helped to keep everyone grounded and connected."

**On Evolving:** "We've been married forty-five years. We have three children and four grandchildren. With lots of therapy and time, we've gotten to a place where we can feel really secure with each other. He was never romantic, but now I get beautiful bouquets every Wednesday. We love each other's company—watching Netflix, cooking dinner, taking walks around the lake. When one person walks in the door, we always sit down across from each other at the table, greet each other warmly, ask if it's a good time to talk. We get in bed at the same time every night and read before turning out the light. I feel deeply blessed and joyfully grateful."

# AND THEN THEY LIVED
## _____ EVER AFTER

"Bring me on board," Bruce says. He clasps his hands across his chest. "Appreciations, please. Three each."

M and I have been seeing Bruce for almost two years. Money problems brought us into couples therapy, life on life's terms has kept us there. I was referred to Bruce by my friend Sam, who, after a series of knock-down, drag-out fights with her husband, started seeing him regularly. "He's really gifted with men," she told me. Getting M to see Bruce was a hard sell; he'd rather do two hundred and four other things before going to a shrink with his wife.

I think Bruce is around sixty-five. He wears button-down shirts and pleated pants. His face is weathered, his eyes pale blue; his voice, clear and firm. Picture Mr. Rogers meets Clint Eastwood. I hardly know anything about him, other than he was once in the Marine Corps in Vietnam and that his wife, an older woman named Pam, likes to dance.

M and I are not looking at each other. I'm looking at Bruce; Bruce is looking at M.

"I don't have any appreciations today, Bruce," I say.

The books in the shelves behind him: *Why We Love, Hold Me Tight, How to Get the Love You Want.*

"Try," Bruce says. He smiles.

I clear my throat.

"Thank you, M, for waking up with the baby in the middle of the night and holding her until she fell back asleep."

"That's one," Bruce says.

"I really appreciate that you called my mom on her birthday and talked with her for ten minutes."

"Two," says Bruce. He presses his fingers together, making a steeple.

We're on the sixth floor of a nondescript building in the Flatiron District. In the reception area: a plastic bowl of wrapped candies and a flat-screen TV that plays staticky episodes of *Batman*.

More silence.

They both turn to me.

"I can't think of anything else," I say.

It's taking all my willpower not to scream about the fact that he forgot to Venmo the housekeeper.

The first year of marriage was sublime. We got a two-bedroom in Greenpoint. Our apartment had a sliver of a patio where we kept bikes and a tiny grill. We'd cook dinner together then walk through the park for ice cream. Our framed ketubah, an illustrated image of two thinly drawn figures walking over a wooden bridge, hung above the kitchen table. We wrote it together, then translated it to Hebrew. *May we never be apart for more than ten days. * May we not spend money frivolously. * May we eat home-cooked dinners together at least three days a week.* The apartment was always spotless. Wherever we were, we were hand in hand. Sometimes I'd fling my arm around his shoulders, half hanging off his neck while we strolled. M and M, joined as one. Like two squares of fabric, woven tight at the seams. I love you, he said. I love you more, I said back. We said it all the time.

"I've got to get back to work," he says.

Loving-kindness and compassion, the root of all Buddhist sutras. Easy in principle; hell to practice. In the second year, the novelty of being newlyweds wore off. Dirty laundry piled up in the hamper. We could never keep track of our money. We paid bills late and screwed up our credit. M's traveling, which slowed when we met, picked up again. He flew to Morocco the first night of Hurricane Sandy and I was pissed. My vows about keeping the refrigerator full and the bath clean and the bed warm were total BS; I was back to my negligent slob ways in no time. We slept sprawled on opposite sides of the bed.

"M still hasn't signed the life insurance paperwork," I say. The second I say it, I regret it.

"Oh god," says M. "The list. That's why she brings me here. To assault me about the list of things I haven't done."

Sometimes therapy is the worst. The drama, the complaining, the shutdown shaggy-haired hipster dad, the emo wife, the sage psychiatrist. All us idiots together, unpacking the psychic cotton of our childhood wounds. Studying the resurfacing of old patterns: miscommunication, resentment, silent scorn, words, words, words, blah, blah, blah. Basically it always comes down to the same thing. Me: *Please please please tell me honestly what's going on in your mind.* M: *Nothing.*

"I brought you here to repair our marriage," I say.

"Let's shift gears." Bruce turns his back to me. "M. What do you want out of this session?"

"I want us to be kind to each other," M says. "There's hardly any kindness between us these days."

Out of the corner of my eye, I see M nodding.

Bruce sighs.

"You two," he says. "It's so obvious you love each other."

We both nod. It's nice to hear it out loud.

Bruce's mentor was Dr. Harville Hendrix, the creator of Imago relationship therapy. Imago is rooted in the belief that we pick our partners unconsciously, based on the traits of our parents. Kids grow up with certain requirements in order to flourish: physical safety, security, opportunities, affection. When those needs go unmet, most likely, later in life, they seek out a life partner who doesn't meet those needs, either. Fights, screams, tears, conflict ensue. According to Hendrix, we can only find our True Self by working through those core issues with our chosen mate.

M says when he walks into the apartment, I hardly ever look up to greet him. I say it kills me when he leaves his ice cream carton on the couch overnight.

M was crazy when I met him. In between jobs, riddled with anxiety and insomnia, he spent the whole springtime convinced he was about to die. A week before our first date, he collapsed on the Williamsburg Bridge, sure he was having a heart attack. A passing cab rushed him to the emergency room. Turns out it was a panic attack. "I'm falling apart," he told me the first time we met for tea, and I loved it. The guy I was dating, scared his heart was literally broken. The whole thing felt like a poem. M's broken heart and me, the girl who would fix it.

"Your grandfather was suffering from a broken heart when we met," I pictured telling our grandchildren one day. "He was scared. I was scared, too. But then we saved each other."

That's where our story started. With the fear. Both of us. Terrified of being left behind. Most of our friends were married by then. They had kids, mortgages. On our first date we walked by a bar, saw a guy sitting alone in front of a beer.

M said, "I'm terrified of becoming that person."

"Me too," I said.

And how he dazzled me. He was a hardcore rock guitarist, a piano prodigy. A history nerd who could recite statistics about every war and president while fixing a car engine or baking a pie. He was buds with all the kids on his block in Brooklyn; the bodega on the corner named a sandwich after him. Had never once raised his voice to his mom. He didn't give a fuck about fashion. He was *that* guy. The one who would help you move your couch, feed your cat when you left town. Every summer, he invited all his friends to his parents' house in Maine for a lobster bake.

*How was your day? Tell me everything. Leave nothing out.* He would say that at the start of every date, the second I got into the car. Before I even had time to put on my seatbelt. *Tell me everything.*

Scared of being alone. Of being torn and raw. All cold bones, no skin. Sutra, suture: They share a root. To sew. To join together.

Love is a verb.

A leap of faith.

I took it with M the day we said: *I do.*

He made me feel safe.

The opposite of faith: fear.

What we're trying to outrun. The two of us, together.

Our third date: We were eating steak frites at Jules Bistro on Eighth Street. I asked how many siblings he had. "There's four of us," M said. "I have an older brother and sister and a younger brother. I'm the lower middle."

"Lower middle!" I screamed out, my mouth full of fries. "I'm the middle, too. This will never work!"

But it did work. For a while. He became my boyfriend. Then he became my husband. We loved together. We lived together. Happily Ever After.

"I'm getting my tooth pulled next week, Bruce." M is talking into his hands. "I can't stop thinking about how weird it is, a permanent piece of my body getting yanked out for good."

Bruce looks at him, sort of blankly.

"He's trying to tell you that he's dying, Bruce." I sigh, roll my eyes. "That's his thing. Any day now, he's just going to drop dead. First his tooth falls out, then his heart stops."

"I must have missed that," Bruce says. "I don't think that's what he's saying. M, do you think you're dying?"

Silence. Then, for the first time all day, M smiles, a small one. His eyes meet mine.

"Absolutely."

I smile back.

Of course I know. I'm his wife. My husband, the hypochondriac. I know what he's thinking.

Oh, M. The man I married. Out of all of them. His hair that sticks up in six different directions, sports-obsessed, early riser, hates olives, loves almonds, former Boy Scout, all-state varsity lacrosse champion, crazy free spirit, loses everything, his ragged, restless soul, eats half a pint of cookie dough ice cream every night. Wears his high school T-shirts to work. OCD about keeping the countertop clean. Loves books about sailing and the Civil War. In college he spent the night in jail for stealing a brass rhinoceros while tripping on acid. Adorable, brilliant, bizarre. The most calm person I know. Kicks ass at work, but can't keep track of the car keys. My friend Tara says I married him because he was the complete opposite of my dad: super mellow, never mean, bad with money. But now those same traits are driving me mad.

The time I said I was craving my mom's baked apples and when I came home from work he was wearing an apron and making them.

When he rolled off the bed while reaching for a book and said: "That was a real wang dang doodle," and we laughed about it for days.

When I sat across from him and cried at the Thai dive bar in Big Sky, Montana, on New Year's Eve.

When we were driving in a whiteout in Colorado. So much snow M couldn't see the road. He was steering based off the GPS screen. Howard Stern on the radio. I was eating pretzels, crinkling my hand in the bag. Had no idea how hard he was concentrating. M snapped. *You need to stop eating those NOW.* We didn't talk for the next three hours.

*Rats.* We said it all the time if something went wrong. *Rats!*

We tried to do the twenty-one-day Goop detox together but only made it to day three.

Our seventh date: He was driving an Aston Martin down Bleecker Street. It was April, late Saturday night. The windows were down, the streets were flooded with people. I said, *I feel sorry for everyone who is not us.* He said, *So do I.*

The press junket in Miami. The first trip we took together out of NYC; I showed up to the airport in overalls and a black bra. On the flight we talked about Shel Silverstein. At dinner M whispered to me what an Irish goodbye was, then headed up to the room first. We had sex for the first time. The next morning, we walked down to the beach while the sun rose. I wore a blue dress. The sky was pink.

"You have to remember that each one of you is doing your best," Bruce says while we're putting our coats on.

The walk to the elevator is always awkward. But there is tenderness between us now. Talk is so hard; thank God for Bruce. In a few hours, we'll meet at home, put our two kids to bed. Our apartment is a mess. Bills, baby bottles, blankets, prescriptions, pacifiers. Most nights, after the kids go to sleep, we'll escape into separate rooms and stare into our phones. This is how it goes: feed kids, close doors, power screens, numb mind, shut down, turn off, go the fuck to sleep. Two people, two doors, two separate lives. The irony: All those years spent in search of one person to pass the time with, and we're still spending it alone.

Sometimes we get a babysitter. We'll see a movie, then walk hand in hand down Bedford, sharing a donut.

Care. It's not a word you think of much, especially when it comes to love. I never thought of it until recently. Love and care. Sounds so geriatric. Ew. Care. I can take care of myself, thank you very much.

But these days, I think about it all the time.

I freaked out the first time I needed to take care of M. The summer before the wedding, he had an operation on his shoulder. I drove him home from surgery down the FDR, while he whimpered in the passenger seat. That night I had to hook up this awkward high-tech ice pack apparatus that the surgeon prescribed, while he moaned on the couch, pale and smelling of hospital. The whole thing made me feel bad, but I didn't know why. The next day I went to the beach and left him alone in the apartment. He was sitting in the dark when I got back.

"I can't believe you left," he slurred, his voice slow from Vicodin.

"I didn't know you wanted me to stay." I was standing in the doorway, holding my sandy bikini. "I wouldn't have known what to do if I did."

Love Hurts. We used to sing it together. In our second bedroom where we jammed all our books, an old TV, two desks, two busted Craigslist club chairs. I was Emmylou Harris; M was Gram Parsons. It's such a beautiful duet; so unironic that it's almost embarrassing. *Love hurts, love scars, love wounds, and mars . . .*

Lust. I want to fuck your brains out.

Desire. I long for you when I'm not with you.

Obsession. I can't stop thinking about you.

I have a recurring fantasy about leaving my husband for this rich photographer who's famous for his fashion campaigns of models in ghosted landscapes. He owns a big vegetable farm upstate. Sometimes I google him at work. Before bed, I imagine our life together. A vivid blur of hot sex, Met galas, summers in Tuscany.

Intimacy. *Let's get cozy under the covers and tell secrets.*

But I don't want to take care of the photographer. I don't want to swab Betadine on his stitches, dab his damp forehead with a cold cloth.

No.

I want him to fuck me black and blue in the back of the bar.

Everyone says you fall in love but I don't agree. Love comes later. You fall into attraction, obsession, lust, desire. You fall into the best version of yourself: the funniest, the skinniest, the smartest. Your legs are shaved, your pussy's waxed, your roots fresh. The table is set: vintage linens, fine china, silver candlesticks. The dress is crisp, pressed, never been worn. Flowers are red, fresh, fragrant. The feast has been prepared and placed before you. My god, the food looks good.

These days, I can take care of M with my eyes closed. Doesn't faze me. Chicken soup, ginger tea, oregano oil, blanket, warm bath, thick socks, a snuggle. *There, there.* I place two acetaminophen on the nightstand, a kiss on his cheek.

Sometimes, though, I wonder: Who's going to take care of me?

I saw the photographer once at a party. He was taller than I remembered, tan, had just returned from some artists' retreat in Palm Springs. Definitely a vibe between us. We talked about meditation, he asked if I believed in God. Stubble on his face, huge hands, eyes pale blue. His breath close and hot.

And then there's love.

Love.

The sex was incredible, that road trip sublime, but now the hormone high, along with mega amounts of adrenaline, cortisol, and serotonin, has subsided. You are back to life as you know it. The difference now is you're in a relationship. But you haven't had time to get your hair done. You didn't get your raise. You are cranky, bloated, and bursting out of your skinny jeans. He's stressed at work. His dick can't get hard. One night, he forgets to pick up Swiffer pads and you stop speaking for a week. You've eaten the feast and the dishes are piled high in the sink. The dress is wrinkled, stained, and you're so sick of wearing it, again and again and again, but it's the only dress you have, so you do. The flowers, no longer fresh, have dried, drained of color. It was all so wonderful, but now it's a mess. The ripe and rabid lust, the sleek and saucy intimacy, the slutty little coquette called desire, must now coexist with the sweet, meek, and humble little thing called love. The practice of being with another person again and again and again. You fuck, you fight, you file a joint tax return, but you can't run.

Love. It's a verb. A thing you make a choice to keep doing. Again and again and again.

Another thing I remember. At some point in the conversation, the photographer started to sound dumb and he was boring me and I was like: *I wish I was talking to M.*

We all get torn apart. But then you get stitched back together, shown your way to the door. You stand, you hope, you wait. For a boy to help guide you down the road. Take your bag, hold your hand. It gets dark and cold on the long walk home.


BRUCE HAS asked each of us to make a list of actions we want the other person to take.

"Things that will make you feel cared for," he says. "It's the small things that make a big difference." He says that when his wife rubs his feet, he feels some sort of primal tenderness that takes him back to childhood. Grosses me out to think of Bruce's feet, but I get it.

This is what's on my list.

*I want you to make me black tea each morning.*
*I want you to read in bed with me three times a week.*
*Once a week I want you to actually read to me.*
*I want us to have a proper Sunday dinner together with candles.*
*    And a roast chicken.*
*Please make an effort to wipe away any stray hairs from the sink*
*    and toilet seat.*
*Tell me I'm beautiful.*
*Let me pick the movie.*
*I want you to open the car door for me.*
*For us to meditate together.*
*Keep the batteries in the box marked* batteries *and the tape in the*
*    box marked* tape.
*I want you to walk me to the subway and hold my hand on the*
*    way.*
*Please be vulnerable. Let me see you.*
*Even though you were not raised Jewish, I need you to celebrate*
*    and host the High Holidays.*
*Please oversee a monthly Excel spreadsheet that details our*
*    overhead and financial projections.*

This is what's on M's list.

*Please just be kind.*


LAST MARCH, during the C-section birth of my second daughter, M sat by my side in the operating room, while, beneath a curtain drawn over the bottom part of my numb body, an obstetrician cut deep into my abdomen. It had been a hard winter. We'd been fighting a lot. My brother and I stopped speaking, my mom was hospitalized, and the weather—with its brutal, relentless blanket of dark cold—had become its own kind of sinister character in our shared story. Fresh starts are rare the older you get and I was really counting on this one—that this child, our new baby, would bring with her a little bit of a new beginning. Hope. We needed some.

It was 12:16 in the afternoon and M had been tasked with the job of DJ'ing the surgery—a mix of our favorites. Neil Young, Lucinda Williams, Bob Dylan. Outside the window of the operating room, the snow was coming down like crazy. We drove to the hospital through a whiteout, ice on the windshield. The night before, I took a break from packing my hospital bag and stood at the window to watch M build a snowman with our daughter, Sunny. I felt full of gratitude and peace. At the home we'd built together. And how far I'd come—how far we'd come—so much life behind us, so much life ahead.

A Nick Cave song came on then. "Rock of Gibraltar," the same song M serenaded me with at our wedding. *Let me say this to you * I'll be steadfast and true * And my love will never falter * The sea would crash about us * The waves would lash about us * I'll be your rock of Gibraltar.*

Then, for some reason, Spotify sputtered and died.

And the room, aside from the *snip-snip-snip* of surgical instruments, went silent.

"Sssh," said M.

He put his hand on my cheek.

In a few minutes the doctor would tug my baby Caroline—pink and screaming and slick with blood—out of my belly. Then she'd stitch me back together. Two halves, once again, made whole. I'd spend the next three days in the hospital. M at my side. Holding my hand, feeding me soup, rubbing salve on my scar. And then we'd go home. Brush our teeth side by side. Hug our kids, climb in bed.

From day to day. From sun to moon. In pain and in joy, in sickness and in health, from life to death, *I do, I do, I do.* This is how you heal. You break, you breathe, you mend. You break again.

"Sing for me, Mike," I said, and he did.

# THANK YOU

Lauren Smythe, first and foremost, for pulling me out of the publishing wreckage of my former life, dusting off my knees, and breathing life into the SFB book. This exists because of you. Alexis Hurley at InkWell, for being the Kris to my Kim. Deeply grateful to Julie Grau for believing in the Power of The Fox from the start, Jess Sindler for being my Book Spirit Guide in Phase One, and Sara Weiss for taking the reins in Phase Two. Cindy Spiegel, Greg Mollica, Barbara Bachman, and Kelly Chian. My big bro and partner-in-crime, Pete Shaps. Rachel Baron, Jordon Goldstein + and the folks at DayGlo, worship you all. Desiree Wichmann, you are the wind beneath my wings. Lucinda Trask, my port in the storm + Rawan Rihani, my gold dust woman. Instagram: I could not have launched SFB without you! Thank you for connecting me to all my foxy followers. Gustaf von Arbin, Ronie Borja, H&H Weddings, Hannah Kelly, Lindsay Bressler, Cole Wilson, Simon Marcus, Julie Schumacher, Heather Andersen, Paula Weber, Mattie Kahn, Isabel McWhorter-Rosen, Sarah Lord, Alex Ronan, Lauryn Small, Lauryn Goldberg, Chris Bernabeo, Josie Miner, Andy Deal, Alexa Wilding, Serena Southam, Elinor Vanderburg, and Noa Griffel. Jacob Rozenberg, Kate Schaefer, Patina Rentals, ABC Carpet and Home, The Wall Group, Magnolia Bakery, Giovanna Randall, Carly Giglio, Stila Cosmetics, Virginia Van Naten, Amanda Lalan. My clients! It's been such an honor to send you down the aisle. Team #guygals: Annie Fuller, Abby Spector, Rachel Bartholomay, Mikey Neff, Becca and Zachary, may Sango the Monkey live long and prosper. Mom and Dad, Viki and John. Lisa, Monday Love for Life. The #thread: LL, SK, MC, MP, TA, RF, the Chicago ladies: DJG, Dana, Brit, Boner, Josie, Aliza, Oona, Leigh. My honorary sisters Marisa + Caroline. Sunny and Coco—if you find this book on a dusty shelf in the year 2041, sorry about the TMI re Daddy's penis. M, always. What a long, strange trip it's been.

# ART CREDITS

Courtesy of Kim Myers Robertson: 130

Courtesy of @bennyfong: 133

Courtesy of Ruvan Wijesooriya: 134

Courtesy of Billy Farrell: 143, 144, 162, 220

Courtesy of Emma Tuccillo: 157

Courtesy of Marko MacPherson: 159

Courtesy of Leilani Bishop: 160

Courtesy of LUCKYGIRL Photography: 164

Courtesy of Jesse Leake: 178

Courtesy of Carrie Goldberg: 180

Courtesy of Rachel Fleit: 181

Courtesy of Joe Schildhorn/BFA.com: 182

Courtesy of Ru Anderson Brown: 189

Courtesy of Jami Saunders: 190, 197

Courtesy of Emily Ullrich: 191

Courtesy of Agaton Strom: 192

Courtesy of Casey Legler: 194

Courtesy of Bryan Cipolla: 195

Courtesy of Richard Tulk-Hart: 198

Courtesy of Luis Escobar: 199

Courtesy of Stories by Joseph Radhik: 200

Courtesy of Weddings by Two/Chris Gifford: 202

Courtesy of John Cary: 203

Courtesy of Adina and Adam: 206 (top)

Courtesy of Bryan Derballa: 206 (bottom)

Courtesy of Kyle Terboss Photography: 207 (top)

Courtesy of Noah Sheldon: 207 (bottom)

Courtesy of Anna Natonewski: 208 (top)

Courtesy of Cynthia Rowley: 208 (bottom)

Courtesy of Liz Ligon: 209

Courtesy of Express/Stringer: 210

Courtesy of Dennis Childers: 222

Courtesy of David Bess: 224, 225

Courtesy of Taste the Style: 226

Courtesy of Becky McNeel: 227

Courtesy of Caroline Connolly: 230

Courtesy of John Chan Photography: 231

Courtesy of Heather Phelps-Lipton: 235

# ABOUT THE AUTHOR

MOLLY ROSEN GUY is the creative director of Stone Fox Bride. She lives in Brooklyn with her family.

stonefoxbride.com

Instagram: @stonefoxbride

Pinterest.com/stonefoxbride

Facebook.com/stonefoxbride

# ABOUT THE TYPE

This book was set in Futura, a typeface designed by Paul Renner (1878–1956) for the Bauer Type Foundry in 1928. The type is simple in design. Futura has a geometric structure and a perfect uniformity of stroke.